The Good Steward Financial Empowerment Series

THE BLACK TAX

The Cost of Being Black in America

And What You Can Do to Help Create the 6 Million Jobs and
1.4 Million Businesses That Are Missing in the Black Community

Shawn D. Rochester, MBA

First Edition
ISBN 978-0-9990072-0-4

Written by Shawn D. Rochester, MBA

Produced and Published by Good Steward Publishing
Address P.O. Box 661, Southbury, CT 06488
Website www.goodstewardliving.com

DEDICATION

To my mother, Joyce, who sacrificed every day
to give my brother and me a better life, in a land of opportunity.

To my aunt, Dorian, a brilliant, funny, selfless, pioneering
educator who transformed the lives of thousands of students
and mentored a generation of educators.

To my aunt, Barbara, whose boundless love, bright smile,
hearty laugh and generous spirit helped to change my life.

To my wife Delores, son Ethan, and daughter Sarah,
you are a gift from God and I love you with all my heart.

To the many researchers who work tirelessly to uncover the truth, who
make great sacrifices to shed light, who toil in obscurity so that others may
gain understanding, and do so not for glory or financial gain, but so that we
may gain knowledge and free ourselves from the tyranny of ignorance.

CONTENTS

Introduction—Why Write a Book Called The Black Tax?

Part 1—The Current Black Tax

Part 2—Historical Black Tax

THE•BLACK•TAX | The Cost Of Being Black In America

If you know the enemy and know yourself, you need not fear the result of a hundred battles. If you know yourself but not the enemy, for every victory gained you will also suffer a defeat. If you know neither the enemy nor yourself, you will succumb in every battle.

— The Art of War, Sun Tzu

THE BLACK TAX

INTRODUCTION

Why Write a Book Called *The Black Tax?*

The Black Tax: The Cost of Being Black in America is Book 2 in The Good Steward Financial Empowerment Series and is a continuation of my first book, *CPR For The SouL: How To Give Yourself a 20% Raise, Eliminate Your Debt and Leave an Inheritance for Your Children's Children.* In *CPR For The SOuL*, I talked about resuscitating our commitment to our SOuL, which is an acronym for Stewardship, Ownership, and Legacy. *Stewardship* is utilizing the limited resources that we have, to their highest and best use, to maximize household cash flow. This is essential to financial stability and empowerment, because everything depends on cash flow—savings, investing, college funds, retirement, start-up costs for new business opportunities or ventures. *Ownership* is paying off all debt to ensure that all assets in your possession are owned by you, *free and clear of all claims.* This is vital because you cannot leave something as an inheritance if you don't own it. *Legacy* is about three things: the first is being able to retire with enough income-generating assets so you can live with dignity. The second is being able to set aside resources so that you can give freely to those who are in need. And the third is being able to leave a sizable inheritance for your children's *children.* The idea is that Stewardship leads to Ownership and ownership ultimately leads to Legacy, which is what I call the SOuL.

Resuscitating our commitment to stewardship, owner-ship, and legacy (SOuL), is where the concept of applying "CPR" to the SOuL comes into play.

The "C" in CPR stands for our *Charge*, which means…
   To seek and apply wisdom, knowledge and understanding
   in order to maximize our resources,
   and leave an inheritance for our children's children.

This *Charge* may seem quite daunting or even downright scary, which is why we supplement our efforts with *Prayer.* That is what the "P" in CPR stands for. It's a *Prayer of Empowerment* that you recite before, during and after your most challenging times on this journey. When you have done all that you can, and when you have gotten to the end of yourself, it's important to remember that it's at that point when God's work is completely and unmistakably clear.

The *Prayer of Empowerment* is as follows:
   Lord strengthen us for we are weary
   and increase our power for we are weak.
   Allow us to put this knowledge into practice and
   rise like the Phoenix from our current situation,
   to transform our lives and the lives of our families
   and to be a blessing to those
   who are the least, last and left out. Amen.

Last, but certainly not least, the "R" in CPR stands for *Responsibility*. While we are in the undesirable position of having very limited resources, scripture says that if you can be trusted with little, you can also be trusted with much. There-fore, our responsibility is to demonstrate that we can be trusted with the little that we have, so that we will be prepared for the overflow that is coming. The word responsibility, while used frequently, is often misunderstood. At the end of the day, taking responsibility is about accepting that what is *required* of you is more important than what is *desired* by you. When we talk about applying CPR, we are talking about applying our *Charge*, our *Prayer of Empowerment*, and taking *Responsibility*.

Ultimately, *CPR for the SOuL* is about managing our resources wisely to generate cash flow and then allocating that cash flow to eliminating debt and leaving a legacy. To do this, we must thoroughly understand everything that affects our cash flow—especially things that reduce it because reductions to cash flow lead to reductions to legacy. The Black tax that African-Americans face in the form of bias greatly reduces our cash flow. This leads us to Book 2, *The Black Tax*.

The Black Tax

Over the last 20 years, I have read various articles about the impact of implicit bias on African-Americans. The research looked at various marketplaces, such as housing, business, finance, the automotive industry, online commerce, and employment. In each article, the often significant costs were based on the findings of studies conducted by researchers at distinguished American universities and institutions. As I read the articles these costs seemed like a series of unjustified taxes on Black Americans. I saved the articles, and decided that at some point in the future I would try to quantify the cumulative effect of those taxes.

Several years later, after almost two decades in Corporate America, I started a financial education and advisory company called Good Steward LLC. As a financial consultant, I help clients develop plans to dramatically increase their household cash flow, eliminate their debt, and set aside enough resources to maximize their income-generating assets during retirement. I also started Good Steward University, where I developed online courses to help Black Americans manage their resources, based on a mindset and a set of actions focused on stewardship, ownership, and legacy.

Within Good Steward University, I developed a course called The Black Tax: The Incremental Cost of Being Black in America. I created that course based on reviewing 25 years of research on the cost of implicit bias on African-Americans. That cost is what I initially called the Black tax. As I researched the findings from a multitude of studies, articles and books, my focus was not on the moral implications of an unjustified "tax" but rather the size and financial impact of that "tax" on Black Americans. This tax is insidious in many ways because it reduces Black Americans' cash flow, thereby reducing our ability to leave a legacy for our children and *their* children. *And unlike other taxes, it provides no positive future benefit whatsoever to Black Americans.* The desire to leave a legacy is a deeply held belief for every Black American regardless of gender, religion, or ethnicity/national origin (e.g., Blacks who have emigrated from countries in Africa, the Caribbean, and South and Central America). This Black tax creates a gap between Black America's desire to leave a legacy and our ability to do so. I wanted to quantify this tax and make people aware of the cost that they are subjected to and are unknowingly paying. I also wanted to inform and arm them with strategies that will help to mitigate that cost.

The findings from reviewing what 25 years of research revealed about the cost of the conscious (explicit) and unconscious (implicit) bias against African-Americans are in Part One: The Current Black Tax. The pervasive, systematic, and omnipotent nature of this Black tax and the current financial condition of Black America begged the question, how did we get here? And how is it that *after 400 years, more than 40 million Black Americans own just 2% of American wealth?* My original intent was to answer this question by attempting to quantify the enormity of the discriminatory forces at work in America that were and are still directed toward African-Americans. I was already aware of the impact of certain discriminatory policies such as "redlining," which channeled billions of dollars of government-sponsored economic support almost exclusively to White families. I decided I would collect and research the effects of other discriminatory policies to help my students understand how unimaginably difficult it was, and still is, for Black Americans to accumulate wealth. I also wanted to illustrate how the deck is consciously and unconsciously stacked against us. I decided to go back to emancipation and look at the research about the economic cost of slavery, Jim Crow, Separate but Equal, the New Deal, and a host of other laws, programs, and policies. In so doing, I found enormous financial costs that were extracted from African-Americans in one long, unrelenting nightmare from slavery to the present day. I found a "tax" of epic and unimaginable proportions, which became Part Two: Historical Black Tax.

Part Three: What Can We Do About the Black Tax? discusses (1) some of the residual impact of the past and current Black Tax and (2) what concerned people—Black, White, and otherwise, can do to help create an environment that will lead to the creation of millions of jobs and businesses within the Black community and dramatically reduce the impact of discrimination against Black Americans. This is a concept called getting your *PHD*, which is an acronym for *Purchase*, *Hire*, and *Deposit*. The fundamental building block of economic development is based on our ability to provide for ourselves and our families, which is in turn based on our ability to earn a decent income. PHD enables economic development because it drives more business with Black enterprises and financial institutions, which in turn increases employment and new business development within the Black community and increases the cost of anti-Black discrimination.

Strategies for Empowerment

I hope the information in *The Black Tax* will (1) increase your knowledge and understanding of the enormity of the unjustified, systematic, financial costs that African-Americans bore and still bear as a result of various forms of anti-Black discrimination, and (2) better position you to engage in serious discussions about the economic effects of anti-Black discrimination. Last, I hope the strategies for financial empowerment in Part Three, Section V: Get Your PHD will empower you to invest in your community, *Purchase* goods and services from Black enterprises, *Hire* Black workers, and *Deposit* your money in Black financial institutions. This will help our $1.2 trillion of annual spending more effectively circulate among Black businesses, financial institutions, and consumers within the Black community; facilitate massive job creation; and build wealth that will financially empower us, decrease our debt, and allow us to leave a legacy.

As is the case with all serious and productive discussions about the financial impact of discrimination against Black Americans, it is wise to consider the following:

- Your feelings and personal experiences are valid. However, if you are not the bearer of this tax (i.e., a Black American) resist putting your feelings, experiences, perceptions, intentions, discomfort, or guilt above the actual cost to, and effect on, those who do bear the tax.

- The vast majority of present-day discrimination is deeply ingrained and often occurs in an unconscious manner. It functions with or without participation, awareness or consent. Your potential lack of awareness does not equal a lack of existence. It simply means that you are not aware of it.

- The costs are real and have had, and still have, a devastating effect on the ability of Black Americans, as a whole, to accumulate the resources necessary to leave a significant inheritance for their children's children.

- The past matters. Your ability to retire with security or fund your children's college education depends on actions and investments that you, your family, or society made many years ago. Black America's current ability to leave a legacy for their children, and to create thriving businesses and healthy communities, was impaired by hundreds of years of continuous discriminatory practices.

- The financial resources extracted from and/or denied to Black Americans were reinvested in institutions, corporations, organizations, and a society that prioritized the economic, political, and social welfare of White Americans above all others. And White Americans benefited, whether or not they were aware of it or approved of it.

- The effects of those discriminatory actions will not dissipate until the amount of work invested in dismantling anti-Black discrimination is equivalent to the amount of work invested in establishing and maintaining it.

Ultimately, we must understand that this is not about whether people are good or bad. People are as good or bad as their actions and "good" people have always done bad things when there were incentives to do so. If you create a mindset based on a perception that there are not enough resources for everyone, or that some people are intrinsically more deserving of resources than others, people will find ways to rationalize accumulating resources for themselves at the expense of others, despite their moral code, faith, or creed. Black America and other interested parties, it is my hope that after reading about the cumulative effects of generations of conscious and unconscious anti-Black biases that have created a discriminatory tax on Black Americans in almost every area—real estate, the automotive market, the job search, online commerce, banking, and business financing—it will make you strongly consider and then ultimately prioritize commercializing Black enterprises and institutions and *not commercializing businesses*, when at all possible, that do not invest in you.✪

PART ONE

THE CURRENT BLACK TAX

What Is a Black Tax?

Black tax is an additional financial strain or heavy burden placed on Black Americans by people and institutions that have conscious and/or unconscious anti-Black biases. The key words here are conscious and unconscious. This tax is placed on Black Americans because of who their fellow citizens "think" they are, (which is dominated by a host of well-documented and unfounded negative stereotypes) not who they actually are.

This tax greatly reduces Black America's ability to invest in new business development, education, housing, employment, and other activities that lead to wealth accumulation. *Very often, the focus is placed on the moral implications of, or the discomfort associated with, discrimination as opposed to the financial costs associated with it.* Because the financial impact of a Black tax affects the wealth of Black Americans, it must occupy a place of primary importance. This is why I focus on the effect that this tax has, and has had, historically, on wealth accumulation in the Black community.

Another important question is, do Americans really harbor anti-Black sentiments? While we are somewhat familiar with the history of anti-Black bias in America, does it still exist today? If so, does it have a meaningful negative financial impact on Black Americans?

In 2012, the Associated Press, working in conjunction with researchers from Stanford University, the University of Michigan, and the University of Chicago, conducted research to understand to what extent Americans have anti-Black bias and how that bias is associated with political affiliation. This question was likely of particular importance, because in 2012 America's first Black president was in the midst of his reelection campaign and the results might have shed some light on how this bias could play out in the election. The results of their research were quite interesting and showed that 51% of Americans expressed explicit anti-Black attitudes and 56% percent of Americans expressed implicit anti-Black attitudes. Republicans had the highest explicit and implicit anti-Black attitudes (80% and 64% respectively). While 32% of Democrats expressed *explicit* anti-Black attitudes, almost twice as many (55%) expressed *implicit* anti-Black attitudes. This means that Democrats harbor far more anti-Black attitudes than they are consciously aware of. With Independents, it was closer to 50/50, which is to say, roughly 50% of Independents had explicit anti-Black bias and 50% had implicit anti-Black bias. Unfortunately, it appears that anti-Black bias, basically ranges from high to very high, depending on political affiliations.

Here are some results from the study...

Proportion of Americans expressing *explicit* anti-Black attitudes was 51% in 2012 (48% in 2008 and 47% in 2010)
- ❒ Proportion of Republicans: 79% in 2012
- ❒ Proportion of Independents: 48% in 2012
- ❒ Proportion of Democrats: 32% in 2012

Proportion of Americans expressing *implicit* anti-Black attitudes was 56% in 2012 (49% in 2008 and 51% in 2010)
- ❒ Proportion of Republicans: 64% in 2012
- ❒ Proportion of Independents: 49% in 2012
- ❒ Proportion of Democrats: 55% in 2012

Before we go any further, let's talk about what explicit and implicit biases are. *Explicit* means that something has been clearly expressed with no room for confusion, and you are fully aware of what was said or done. Bias is a systematic error in judgment. For instance, continually thinking a certain type of person is a criminal when they are no more likely to be a criminal than anyone else. To determine a person's *explicit bias*, the researchers would ask that person direct questions about race. For example: "Do you think that the impact of 250 years of slavery had a negative impact on the current position that Black Americans are in today?" That is clearly a question about race. *An implicit bias* refers to attitudes and/or stereotypes that affect our understanding, actions, and decisions in an unconscious manner. It is bias you harbor in your *unconscious* mind that is not accessible to you through introspection and reflection.

Because people are not aware of their implicit biases, researchers have developed clever ways to get an understanding of the presence of those biases. They might show their subjects pictures or diagrams that have nothing to do with race, and ask how they feel (positively or negatively) about the picture or diagram. But before they show them the non-racial picture or diagram, they will randomly show the person a picture of a Black male or a White male, and then ask them how they feel about the non-racial diagram. It often turns out that people who have an anti-Black bias feel more negatively about the picture, after seeing a Black male, and more positively about the diagram after seeing a White male. The researcher will do this over and over with different subjects and use statistical methods to figure out the level of bias across the sample.

Think about it this way: They're asking people how they feel about a picture/diagram that has nothing to do with race but their feelings about those images are affected by their feeling toward the image of a Black male or White male that precedes the image they are actually focused on. When the researchers in this Associated Press study completed their work, they found that almost *six out of every 10 Americans had anti-Black attitudes*.

Researchers at Harvard University have long studied the effects of implicit bias and created an online Implicit Association Test (IAT) to measure biased attitudes and beliefs that people are unwilling or unable to report. While taking an IAT for race, a person must categorize "good" and "bad" words with images of Black and White people. The more quickly the person can associate positive words with "White people" or

"Black people" the stronger their implicit preference for that group. The race IAT has been taken by over 3.3 million people between 2002 and 2015 and researchers have found that *almost 70% of Americans have an implicit preference for White people over Black people*. The data also shows that *only 2% of Americans have a strong implicit preference for Black people*. This is not surprising, given the strong negative stereotypes associated with Black people in American society, coupled with a long history of several hundred years of intense racial discrimination.

Considering this, the answer to the question "do Americans still harbor anti-Black biases?" is a resounding yes. *The vast majority of Americans harbor high levels of both conscious and unconscious bias against African-Americans.* Since we know that biases (implicit and explicit) can manifest themselves in the actions and decision-making of those who hold them, the next logical step is to understand the extent to which these biases manifest as a tax on Black Americans.

Black Tax in the Real Estate Market

The American Dream includes the goal of home ownership. The first step in securing the American Dream is to look for a home. Let's see what research says about the African-American experience during the home-search process. In 2011, a National Association of Realtors study found that the average search for a new home takes about 12 weeks and during that search the average person will look at 12 homes. However, if you're Black your search is going to take longer and you're going to see fewer homes. The study found that *Black Americans are told about almost 20% fewer homes and then are shown almost 20% fewer homes as compared to Whites*. So, if a White homebuyer is told about 10 homes, a Black homebuyer will likely be told about eight, and shown even fewer homes. This clearly makes it harder to find your dream home, because if you're not told about a home or shown a home, it won't be under consideration during your buying process. This is not only discriminatory; but it also costs more of your time, which means you have less time for other productive pursuits. While it is clearly a tax on your time, which also reduces your options, it is a tax that is difficult to quantify.

Let's assume that despite the inconvenience of having to allocate more time than your peers to the search process, you've managed to find your dream home and you're ready for the next step, which is seeking financing. The Journal of Urban Economics published a study in 2016[1] that examined the extent to which discrimination still exists in the lending industry for residential real estate. *They found that people who inquired about getting mortgage financing, who had African-American-sounding names, were less likely to receive a response by Mortgage Lending Organizations (MLOs) than people who had White-sounding names. When people who had African-American-sounding names did receive a response from the MLOs, it was a less preferential response than people who had White-sounding names.* You may be tempted to think that the people with Black-sounding names had worse credit and therefore got less of a response, but this was not the case. The potential applicants all had similar credit scores and credit history. Researchers found that the level of discrimination was quite high for a characteristic (race) that *should not* matter, relative to one that *should* matter significantly (credit score).

As we discussed in *CPR for the SOuL*, credit scores are very important. That simple three-digit number summarizes a person's credit history and is meant to provide a strong indication of whether or not a borrower is likely to repay his or her debts. In fact, 65% of the factors that go into a FICO score characterize the extent to which a person has been paying their debt as required and the extent to which they are utilizing the credit that has been extended to them. Not only did the folks in the study have similar credit scores, but they also had similar payment histories, utilization rates (how much of their credit they used), and types of credit. Yet the borrowers with Black-sounding names were treated quite differently. In fact, the extent of the difference in the treatment between the applicants with White-sounding names and Black-sounding names had the same impact as if the applicants with Black-sounding names had FICO scores that were 71 points lower[2]. *That is a massive difference in credit score and could easily lead to outright denial or substantially higher interest rates over the life on a loan.* Can you imagine having good credit yet being treated as if you have poor credit? That is a truly discriminatory and excessive tax. Another study by the Economic Policy Institute also found that Black Americans with a 660 FICO credit score were three times more likely to receive a high interest rate mortgage (i.e., an interest rate that is 1.5% higher than what they should get based on their credit score) than White Americans with a 660 FICO score. A 1992 study by the Federal Reserve Bank of Boston also found that:

> "...even after controlling for financial, employment, and neighborhood characteristics, Black and Hispanic mortgage applicants in the Boston metropolitan area

are roughly 60 percent more likely to be turned down than Whites. This discrepancy means that minority applicants with the same economic and property characteristics as White applicants would experience a denial rate of 17 percent rather than the actual White denial rate of 11 percent. Thus, in the end, a statistically significant gap remains, which is associated with race."[3]

So far, we've seen that if you're Black (1) during the process of looking for a home you're more likely be told about fewer homes and shown fewer homes. (2) When you inquire about getting a loan and have an African-American-sounding name you're more likely to be treated as if your credit worthiness is substantially lower than it is. (3) After you have submitted your application, you are 60% more likely to be turned down than Whites with similar characteristics. (4) You're three times more likely to receive a higher-priced loan than your White counterpart with the same credit risk. It seems like a pattern is emerging that shows a significant difference in treatment of and costs to African-Americans. If the researchers are correct then we should be able to find evidence of this tax in the marketplace.

Below are examples of some large American banks that were sued by the U.S. Justice Department for discriminating against minority homebuyers.

Bank of America, which is a massive bank, was sued by the Justice Department and ultimately paid $335 million[4] to settle the lawsuit. Bank of America had *overcharged 200,000 minority borrowers with higher rates and fees than White customers with the same credit score.* This was not an issue of a minority borrower having a lower score and subsequently receiving a higher interest rate, which is what one might expect. It was a matter of hundreds of thousands of borrowers being given interest rates that were far higher than they otherwise should have been. In fact, Bank of America's Countrywide Financial division steered Black and Latino borrowers into high-risk, subprime loans with draconian rates and terms, even though they qualified for prime rates. *These borrowers wound up paying tens of thousands of dollars more, including up-front costs, than their White counterparts with similar credit risk.*

Wells Fargo, another massive bank, was also sued by the Justice Department and paid $175 million to settle accusations that its independent brokers discriminated against Black and Hispanic borrowers.[5] Wells Fargo *charged 30,000 minority buyers higher interest rates and higher fees associated with borrowing than White borrowers with the same credit risk.* They also steered 4,000 minority borrowers into costly interest-rate subprime loans, while White borrowers with the same credit risk were given prime-rate loans. In Chicago, Black borrowers paid almost $3,000 more in fees for a $300,000 loan than White borrowers with the same credit risk. Wells Fargo was so aggressive, according to Elizabeth Jacobson, one of the bank's top-producing subprime loan officers, that Wells Fargo (1) paid its loan officers three to four times more for subprime loans than for prime loans, (2) had a goal of having the subprime division pay the entire fixed cost for the entire company, and (3) specifically targeted Black churches because it figured that Black churches had a lot of influence and could convince congregants to take out subprime loans.

Now let's suppose that you've completed the home acquisition process, and you're now a newly minted homeowner. The majority of your personal and household net worth will be the value of your home. In fact, the vast majority of the net worth of American households come from their homes. This is particularly true of Black Americans, where 64% of their net worth is from real estate holdings, whereas only 39% of White household wealth is driven by real estate holdings. So, the value of real estate is vital for African-American wealth accumulation. More specifically, the increase in value over time, which is called *appreciation*, is vital to African-American wealth accumulation.

The difference between what your home is worth and what you owe on it is called your equity in the home. *Equity* is the financial value assigned to the portion of the home that you own. A *Forbes* article written by Dorothy Brown, professor of tax law at Emory University School of Law, [6] indicated that *as the percentage of Black people in a neighborhood increases beyond 10%, a gap in appreciation begins and continues as the percentage of Black people increases*. Even when researchers control for, or take into account, age, social class, household structure and geography, the appreciation gap persists and continues to increase as the percentage of Black people increases. Researchers from George Washington University found that *Black homeowners receive 18%[7] less value for their homes per dollar of income than White homeowners*. A gap also clearly exists between Black and White neighborhoods with equal income levels.

In one survey, researchers found that *Whites reported they will be unlikely to purchase a home in a predominantly Black neighborhood even if it met their requirements in terms of price, rooms, safety, and school system*. Another study found that "the presence of African-Americans in a neighborhood resulted in a downgrading of its desirability"[8] for Whites, regardless of economic status of the neighborhood. Yet another found that "Whites avoid living in neighborhoods with a non-token (more than only a few) Black population because of the associations they make between the presence of Blacks and high crime, low housing values, and low-quality education. But if these factors were not the case in actuality or in Whites' perceptions, Whites would continue to be negatively influenced by Black neighborhood composition."[9]

This is not only remarkable, it is also indicative of a significant anti-Black bias because even with all of these positive attributes, *the mere presence of a substantial representation of African-Americans diminishes the desire to live in a neighborhood* that has a "non-token" presence of Black Americans. Since 1970, only 2%[10] of White Americans have moved from predominantly White neighborhoods to predominantly Black neighborhoods. *The collective effect of a group that controls over 90%[11] of all wealth in the country, to not buy homes in neighborhoods where African-Americans live, puts a significant negative economic impact on real-estate values in almost all Black neighborhoods* (irrespective of income levels) in the country. This impact dramatically reduces the ability of African-American homeowners to accumulate wealth and leave a legacy.

As you can see, the Black tax in the real-estate market starts small and somewhat innocuously, then increases dramatically. If you are African-American, you will likely have to spend more time looking for a home and securing financing. This portion of the tax is more difficult to quantify because it reduces the amount of time that you have for your family, church, business, and employment. You are also more likely to be denied a loan. If you do receive a loan, you are more likely to be charged higher fees and interest rates than your White peers with similar credit histories. Let's take a look at the numbers. Suppose you purchase a home for $450,000. Since you are three times more likely to receive a loan with higher interest than is actually consistent with your credit worthiness, you could receive an interest rate that could *cost you an additional $144,000 over the life of the loan*. If you are also charged higher fees ($3,000 using the Wells Fargo model), *that could cost you an additional $13,000 over the life of the loan*. And if you purchased your home in a neighborhood with a Black population above 10%, (and most Black Americans live in such neighborhoods) you could end up with your home being worth 18% less than it otherwise would be, due to the appreciation gap. That could amount to $190,000 after 30 years. Cumulatively, *it's possible to pay a Black tax that could cost you an additional $345,000 on the purchase of your home*, which is truly extraordinary.

If you think about the impact of the appreciation gap on African-Americans,

> **"If you are African - American, you will likely have to spend more time looking for a home and securing financing....You are also more likely to be denied a loan. If you do receive a loan, you are more likely to be charged high- er fees and interest rates than your White peers with similar credit histories. "**

the tax becomes massive. African-Americans own an esti- mated $1.4 trillion of real estate and the vast majority of that real estate is in communities where African-Americans are more than 10% of the population. This means that *Black Americans could (in total) have $317 billion less real-estate value than they otherwise should*. This is a truly massive and crippling tax on Black people and certainly underscores the need for Black Americans to bank with Black financial institutions to avoid the discriminatory effects of institutions that have long had conscious or unconscious predatory relationships with the Black community.

Black Tax in the Automotive Market

Economists Ian Ayres and Peter Siegelman[12] conducted a study to understand if there are differences in how dealerships treat potential car buyers of different races. The study focused on the negotiating process associated with 300 potential car purchases in the Chicago area. What they found was that dealers offered Black male testers significantly higher prices than White male testers, even when the testers used identical bargaining strategies. As a matter of fact, the salesmen gave White buyers an initial price that was *43% lower* than the initial price they gave Black male buyers before any negotiations took place. To be clear: The final price that was negotiated by Black buyers was higher than the initial price given to White buyers *before the White buyers even began negotiating*. At the end of the negotiations, *Black male buyers wound up paying an average of $1,100 more than their White male counterparts*. Potential Black buyers also paid higher prices in White suburbs than in the inner city. The researchers had a tough time accounting for the difference in pricing and speculated that perhaps the salesmen thought that White buyers were more informed about the profit margin than Black buyers and just volunteered more of a price break to the White buyers. Given that anyone who needs a car will likely buy at least seven of them over the course of his or her life, there is a significant opportunity for Black buyers to incur astounding incremental costs while White buyers receive incredible *unearned* benefits.

Since cars, like homes, are big-ticket items that few people can afford to buy outright, most people will need financing. The National Consumer Law Center looked at millions of auto loans nationwide from the 1990s and 2000s to investigate the existence of race based discrepancies within the auto-financing market. Their *study found widespread racial disparities, unrelated to credit risk, in the markups added by auto dealers to a borrower's auto loan rate.* What many consumers don't know is that auto dealerships are often given discretion to markup interest rates on auto loans before passing them on to their customers. This means the dealer *can increase your interest rate solely at their discretion, which increases their profit margin and they're under no obligation to tell you about it.* The study also found statistically significant markups on auto loans for African-Americans in every state and every region of the country where there was data.

The *markups for Black borrowers ranged from 110% to 454% over the markup given to White borrowers with the same credit risk.* Think about it this way: The financing company might tell the auto dealer that they are willing to finance your purchase with a 5% APR, but the dealer marks it up to 5.5% and tells you that your rate is 5.5% and that's the best they can do while giving a White borrower with the same credit risk a 5% interest rate. Unless you have additional information, you'll assume that they are doing all they can to get you the best rate and you might take it. Why? Cars are very emotional purchases that can affect how friends, peers, associates, and society at large might perceive you. And when you mix emotion and lack of information within the buying process for expensive items, it becomes easy to get taken advantage of and not even know it. *Discriminatory markups can cost Black buyers an additional $400 to $500 per year.* As we have seen with the Black tax in the re-al-estate market, if the researchers are correct we should also be able to quantify the effects of discriminatory practices in the marketplace.

Below is a list of auto companies that have been sued by the Justice Department for charging Black automotive bor-rowers higher rates than their White counterparts with similar credit risk.

2016 Toyota—Sued by Justice Department—Paid $22M

❐ Dealers charged Black buyers 0.27% more interest than Whites with *similar credit risk*

2014 Honda—Sued by Justice Department—Paid $24M

❐ Dealers charged Black buyers more interest than Whites with *similar credit risk*

2013 Ally Financial (formerly GMAC)—Sued by Justice Department—Paid $98M

❐ Dealers charged Black buyers 0.25% more interest than Whites with *similar credit risk* (235,000 car buyers were overcharged)

2015 Fifth Third Bank—Sued by Justice Department—Paid $18M

❐ Banks charged Black and Hispanic buyers more interest than Whites with *similar credit risk* (24,500 car buyers were overcharged)

In the list above, GMAC's (currently Ally Financial) transgressions were particularly egregious. A study by Vanderbilt business professor Mark Cohen found that *Black borrowers from GMAC paid an average of $1,229 in extra interest over the life of a loan*, compared with the average of $867 paid by Whites (42% more). The discrepancies were so widespread that even Black General Motors employees paid more than their White counterparts to get a loan. In addition to higher comparative interest rates, Black customers are also less likely to be offered preferential interest rates. Black college graduates were also less likely to be offered below-market interest rates on car loans for recent college graduates. Cohen's report claims that *GMAC borrowers were charged a total of $421.6 million in subjective markups and nearly 20% was paid by Blacks even though they were only 8.5% of GMAC borrowers.*

Black Tax in the Auto Insurance Market

Let's assume that you've purchased a car and have avoided those additional discriminatory costs. By law, you will need automobile insurance, which is a substantial annual cost for most drivers. Let's see what researchers have to say about discrimination in the auto insurance market. A 2015 report released by the Consumer Federation of America[13] found that *a female driver with a perfect driving record could pay significantly more for car insurance if she lives in a predominantly African-American community rather than a mostly White one, even when all other factors are equal.* The report also found that the driver was charged 77%

more if the community was a predominantly African-American, low-income neighborhood as opposed to a predominantly White, low-income neighborhood. If on the other hand, the driver lived in an upper-middle income predominantly Black neighborhood, *she was charged 194% more than if the community was predominantly White.* The findings from this study indicate that even though the driver has a perfect driving record, her costs will increase dramatically depending on the amount of Black people that live around her, regardless of the economic status of the community. This is an extraordinary financial burden placed on Black people who live in predominantly Black communities and the non-Black car owners who also live in those communities.

Let's run the numbers: Research indicates that if you are Black you're more likely to pay (1) a higher purchase price, (2) higher financing costs, and (3) higher insurance premiums, even if you have a perfect driving record but live in a Black community. Since most people will own at least seven cars over their lifetimes, *the accumulative cost of this level of discrimination could cost up to $70,000 over the course of a lifetime.*

Given that Black Americans purchase or lease about 5 million cars per year, the aggregate cost could be substantial.

- $1,100: average increase in purchase price could cost Black Americans up to $5.5 billion per year

- An additional $500 of interest per year could cost up to $2.5 billion per year of incremental interest cost

- An additional $500 of insurance premium per year could cost up to $2.5 billion per year of incremental insurance cost

Taken as a whole, this could cost African-Americans up to $10 billion per year in incremental automotive costs. Think about the discriminatory financial fees being levied against African-Americans through higher purchase prices, higher financing costs and higher insurance costs. This is a Black tax of epic proportions, which significantly reduces Black America's ability to leave a legacy for our children's children.

Black Tax in Online Commerce

There is clearly a Black tax within the pillars of the American Dream, which are the housing and automotive markets. But what about the new frontier of online commerce? Well, researchers from Harvard's Business School had the same question so they conducted a study in 2014 to get a sense of the extent to which discrimination is present in online commerce.

They looked at Airbnb, which is an online company that allows people to rent out their homes, or rooms within their homes to various travelers. Airbnb provides an alternative to staying at a hotel. If you have a room available you can post it on the site. People who are looking for a room in your area can then rent it from you. It's a very innovative idea and the service is available in the United States and in many other countries.

The researchers found that Black hosts on Airbnb got significantly lower rates than non-Black hosts, even with comparable locations, rooms, and amenities. In fact, *for comparable offerings, Black hosts got an average rate of $107 while non-Black hosts got an average rate of $144.* This amounts to a 35% differential in price, which is huge. But why would there be such a difference in price? Even if renters do have a bias, what would cause it to emerge? Well, it turns out that Airbnb requires people who are renting rooms or homes to create a profile with their picture. The profile picture makes potential renters aware of the owner's race and allows conscious and unconscious bias to manifest in the pricing differential. Researchers also created 20 user profiles and sent rental requests to roughly 6,400 hosts. *Rental requests with Black-sounding names were 16% less likely to be accepted than those with White-sounding names.* The discrimination was pervasive and occurred whether Blacks were buyers or sellers of rental space, occurred with cheap listings and expensive ones, in diverse neighborhoods and homogeneous ones, in rooms in the host's own dwelling and in separate units rented out by landlords with multiple listings.[14] *This tax appears to exist whenever people with anti-Black bias become aware that the person they are dealing with is African-American.*

Researchers from Harvard and Yale Law School[15] also conducted a study to better understand the extent to which discrimination plays a role in certain aspects of online commerce. The researchers were quite clever, and looked at the value that buyers placed on baseball cards in an eBay online auction. This auction format was well-suited to isolating racial effects because the potential bidders did not have information on the appearance or socioeconomic background of the sellers. The researchers found that *baseball cards from African-Americans sellers were offered a price that was 20% lower than the same cards that were being sold by White sellers.* That's right, the same card received a substantially different offer. But why would this happen? If buyers were discriminating, what would trigger it? Research showed that when the buyer looked at the picture of the baseball card he or she could see the fingers of the seller holding the card. In some instances, buyers saw the same baseball card, being held by Black fingers, and in other instances the same card was being held by White fingers. *The skin color of the fingers allowed anti-Black bias to be triggered and it was expressed in the form of lower prices for Black sellers.* Think deeply about that, the mere presence of Black skin in the photo led to a lower value for the item.

Black Tax in the Job Search

While you may not spend much time renting rooms or offering rooms for rent on Airbnb, or even selling merchandise on eBay, you will probably have to look for a job at some point in your career. In 2002, two researchers from the University of Chicago published a groundbreaking study that examined discrimination in the labor market.[16] The report was titled "Are Emily and Brandon More Employable Than Lakisha and Jamal?" To help them get the necessary data, the researchers created a set of resumes, which they varied in terms of quality. For their purposes, "quality" represented the years of experience in an industry or function, the level of education, and/or the caliber of the educational institution where the credentials were earned. Quality therefore should matter quite a bit. The researchers then randomly assigned names to resumes of the same quality; some came from Emily, some from Lakisha, some were from Brandon, and some from Jamal. Again, we're talking about the same resumes and the same quality, *just different names*. The researchers then responded to various help-wanted ads in Boston and Chicago.

What the *researchers found was that resumes with the White-sounding names (i.e., Emily or Brandon) received 50% more callbacks.* Now think about that. If you don't get a callback, you can't have a conversation about your qualifications to convince the potential employer that you would be right for the job. *They also found that resumes with Black-sounding names would need eight more years of additional work experience to have the same likelihood of getting a call back as a resume with a White-sounding name.* Imagine, to counter the bias triggered by having a Black-sounding name, *you would need eight more years of experience.*

The researchers also found that as they increased the quality of the resumes with the White-sounding names, the callbacks went up by 30%. This makes sense; stronger credentials should increase an employer's level of interest.

> "...researchers found that the resumes with the White-sounding names (i.e., Emily or Brandon) received 50% more callbacks"

However, when they looked at the resumes with African-American names (i.e., Lakisha and Jamal) they found that as they increased the quality of the resume, there was a negligible impact on callbacks. While this is truly remarkable and to some extent completely nonsensical, it is consistent with a study conducted by Public/Private Ventures, a nonprofit research organization. Public/Private Ventures conducted a study[17] on a yearlong training program, which helped participants develop skills valued by employers in specific industries. After the yearlong program, women, Hispanic and foreign-born participants all experienced higher employments rates. However, while the skills of the African-American participants increased after the yearlong training, their employment rates did not.

Apparently, the characteristics that should matter most (experience, education and expertise) have no impact, but your name, which should not matter at all, had a high impact. The University of Chicago researchers also found that *the level of discrimination was significant and uniform across industry and occupation, size, or whether or not the employer claims to be an equal opportunity employer.* What adds to the level of absurdity is that Jamal is of Arabic origin and means "beautiful" and Lakisha has roots in the Swahili language and means "favorite one". But in America, Blacks are not only discriminated against based on our names, we are also required to have eight more years of work experience than our White counterparts to get a callback. The level of discrimination during the job search is so high that researchers from Arizona State University[18] found that White job applicants with a felony conviction get more callbacks than Black job applicants with no criminal record at all. A heavy Black tax indeed.

Black Tax in the Legal Profession

You've finally completed the job search and you're in one of the most sought-after occupations in the country. You're an associate at a large law firm. You're highly educated, hardworking, motivated, and excited about being able to advance in your chosen field and you're looking forward to accumulating significant financial resources to leave an inheritance for not only your children, but also your *children's* children. To what extent does discrimination play a role in your ability to do that? Nextions' research and consulting firm conducted an experiment to see if there is discernible discrimination in the legal field.

Nextions created a legal memo and inserted 22 errors in the memo. Seven errors were from minor spelling or grammar mistakes, six errors were substantive technical writing mistakes, five errors were errors in fact, and four of the errors were from the analysis of the facts. Nextions then sent the memo to 60 partners at 22 large law firms. Half of the partners were told that the memo they received was written by an associate named Thomas Meyer an African-American, and the remaining partners were told that the memo was written by an associate named Thomas Meyer, who was Caucasian. The memos that each partner received were exactly the same, the name of the associate was the same, and the name was also a Caucasian-sounding name. The only difference was that one group of partners thought that Thomas Meyer was Black and the other group thought that Thomas Meyer was White.

Nextions examined the results and found that the average grade for the "Caucasian" lawyer was a 4.1 out of 5; however, the average grade for the "African-American" lawyer *was 3.2 out of 5,* which is essentially a failing grade for any high-achieving lawyer. *The partners who thought that Thomas Meyer was Black, not only gave him a dramatically lower score but also had lower predictions for his success as a lawyer.* So, the Black lawyer receives a failing grade and the White lawyer receives a passing grade *for the same memo* and a much higher appraisal of his future success as a lawyer.

Nextions also reported that the partners found an average of 2.9 out of seven spelling and grammar errors in the memo written by the White Thomas Meyer and 5.8 out of seven errors in the memo by the African-American Thomas Meyer.

Let's think about this carefully. *When the memo appeared to be from a Black lawyer the partners found almost 100% more errors than they found for the White lawyer.* How unfortunate for the Black lawyer and very fortunate for the White lawyer. Fewer technical writing and factual errors were also found in the memo by the supposedly White author. Can you imagine being a Black lawyer at a top law firm, where everyone is sharp and hardworking, but your work, even though it's the same as your White counterparts, gets 100% more scrutiny. The fundamental problem is much more than the injustice; it's the massive tax on the Black lawyer. *If the Black lawyer is unable to get on a track to become partner because of this kind of bias, even though the quality of his work is the same as his White peers, this could cost the Black lawyer $11 million in earnings over the course of his career.*

"Partners at large law firms will often find 100% more mistakes in legal memos if they believe that the author of the memo is a Black lawyer versus when they think the same memo is written by a White lawyer."

This is an extraordinary tax to pay for an irrational bias that has nothing to do with the quality of a person's work. It is also important to note that only 2% of partners at major law firms are Black and less than 3% of all lawyers are Black. Perhaps this tax is a driving force behind those numbers.

What about other high-growth, higher-earnings fields? A 2016 report[19] by the British Medical Journal, found that White male physicians earn 35% more than Black male physicians in the United States, even after accounting for the total hours worked, experience and specialty. A 35% earnings gap means that Black physicians are earning $65,000 less per year than their White peers ($253,042 for White male physicians versus $188,230 for Black male physicians). Assuming a 35% tax rate and a 5% internal rate of return (IRR), this Black-White earnings gap could cost a Black male doctor $2.9 million over a 30-year period. A 2008 report[20] from the American College of Healthcare Executives (ACHE), found that taking into account the educational level attained and years of healthcare management experience, White men earned a median of $168,200 in 2007; while Black men earned $142,400 or 15% less than White men. *That's a $26,000-per-year difference in income, which could amount to $1.2 million of after-tax income over 30 years (assuming a 35% tax rate and a 5% internal rate of return, IRR).* Hire.com also found that *Black software engineers are the least well-paid* with the average salary being up to 8.6% less than their White colleagues ($115k compared to $125k). *That amounts to a $10,000-per-year difference or $450,000 over 30 years (assuming a 35% tax rate and 5% IRR).* That's a high tax for Black doctors, executives, and engineers to pay.

Black Tax in Business Financing

A 1998 study[21] conducted by professors at Dartmouth College, Wellesley College and Williams College looked at discrimination in the Small Business Credit Market and found that *Black-owned firms are twice as likely to be denied credit despite credit worthiness, as White-owned firms.* All things being equal, this means that Black-owned firms receive less credit than their credit worthiness would dictate. Black entrepreneurs also have far less capital and access to capital than White entrepreneurs when starting and growing a business. The amount of capital available to a business owner is a primary factor in determining whether a business will fail or succeed. Despite the obvious capital handicap that Black businesses have relative to White business owners, they are denied access to capital at higher rates than their White counterparts who have similar credit worthiness and far more access to capital. Researchers also found that the *interest rates charged to Black-owned businesses were close to 1% higher than the rates charged to White-owned businesses despite credit worthiness.* Therefore, not only are Black-owned businesses being denied credit more frequently, when they are extended credit the interest is higher than White-owned businesses with the same credit.

Research also found that Black businesses paid higher rates across credit levels. For example:

- ❐ Black businesses with poor credit were charged higher rates than White businesses with the same/similar credit profile
- ❐ Black businesses with fair/good credit were charged higher rates than White businesses with the same/similar credit profile
- ❐ Black businesses with excellent credit were charged higher rates than White businesses with the same/similar credit profile

This follows the same trend in the residential mortgage

market.

Fifteen years later, in 2013 the Small Business Administration (SBA)[22] conducted another study which found that *minority business owners of young firms were significantly less likely to have their loan applications approved than were similar White business owners, even after taking into account factors such as industry, credit score, legal form, and human capital.* The results also suggested that Blacks and Hispanics relied less than Whites on formal financing channels such as bank financing, even after considering creditworthiness and wealth levels. This of course makes sense, since they are being denied more often than they should be and are being charged higher rates than their credit requires. This tax on Black-owned businesses is particularly significant because Black-owned businesses employ about 6 million[23] fewer people than they otherwise should, based on the population of Black Americans as a percentage of the total U.S. population. Clearly, the negative impact reverberates throughout the community. The funding challenge associated with Black businesses is so stark that in 2007, Black-owned small businesses received *less than 2%[24] of all loan money distributed through the SBA.* This is further supported by a Pepperdine Private Capital Access Index report[25] that found that only 1% of the certified African-American-owned businesses they sampled were able to procure an SBA-backed loan.

The Black Tax Is Pervasive

The research is clear. With almost six out of every 10 Americans having anti-Black attitudes and almost seven out of 10 having an unconscious preference for White people over Black people, there is indeed a substantial bias against Black Americans. That bias manifests itself as a tax that extracts billions of dollars' worth of financial resources from African-American households and dramatically reduces those households' ability to leave a significant legacy.

In the housing market, we've seen that if you're Black (1) you're more likely be told about fewer homes and shown fewer homes when you are looking for a home. (2) You're also more likely to be treated as if your credit worthiness is substantially lower than it actually is if you have an African-American-sounding name. (3) You are 60% more likely to be turned down for a loan than Whites with similar characteristics. (4) You are three times more likely to receive a higher-priced loan than your White counterpart with the same credit risk. (5) Your home could end up being worth 18% less than it otherwise should if you live in an area where the Black population is more than 10% of the total population. For a home purchased by an African-American for $450,000, the increased interest rate, fees, and the long-term equity appreciation gap could cost an additional $345,000 over 30 years. *For Black Americans, the equity-appreciation gap alone could be reducing their real estate holdings by $317 billion.*

We've also seen similar costs to Black Americans in the auto market. An African-American buyer is more likely to pay

(1) a higher purchase price, (2) higher financing costs, and (3) higher insurance premiums even if you have a perfect driving record but live in a Black community. Since most people will likely own at least seven cars in their lifetimes, this level of discrimination could cost a Black buyer up to $70,000 over the course of their life. Given that Black Americans purchase or lease about 5 million cars per year, the combined cost could be up to *$10 billion per year in incremental automotive costs.*

In the online market the mere presence of Black skin, or an African-American-sounding name, can lower the value of what vendors are selling by 20% to 35%. In the job market, a resume with an African-American-sounding name can get 50% fewer callbacks for interviews than the same resume with a White-sounding name and requires up to eight more years of work experience to compensate for the Black-sounding name. Partners at large law firms will often find 100% more mistakes in legal memos if they believe that the author of the memo is a Black lawyer versus when they think the same memo is written by a White lawyer. They will also see less likelihood for future success as a lawyer when the same memo is thought to be written by a Black attorney. The consequence of not achieving the position of partner at a large firm because of this kind of bias could cost a Black lawyer *$11 million in lifetime earnings.* The earnings gap between Black and White software engineers and Black and White health-care executives could cost Black employees between $450,000 to $1,000,000 respectively. And despite having less capital to start a business than their White counterparts, Black business owners are denied credit more frequently and charged higher interests than White-owned businesses with the same credit. *Researchers, have* *estimated that because of the cost of discrimination in securing loans for homes and businesses, African-Americans are losing an estimated $100 billion in equity over this current generation as compared to their White counterparts.*[26]

In Part One we explored the concept of the Black tax and attempted to quantify some of the ways that this tax is driven by conscious and unconscious anti-Black bias, and how it creates a significant, additional, financial burden on Black American households. The research discussed in this part of the book is by no means exhaustive and the industries that were highlighted are but a subset of the markets and institutions, like the criminal justice, educational and healthcare systems, where African-Americans are subjected to additional financial burdens. ✪

*Men ... avenge themselves for slight offenses
but cannot do so for grave ones; so the offense
one does to a man should be of such [magnitude]
that one does not fear revenge for it.*

—*The Prince, Niccolò Machiavelli*

HISTORICAL BLACK TAX

How Did We Get Here?

I n Part One, we examined the large and pervasive tax that Black Americans face due to the implicit and explicit anti-Black bias of their fellow citizens. This tax exists in almost every market where people are required to make decisions that affect the price of various goods and services that are consumed by Black Americans. Research shows that it is quite prevalent in the housing market, the automotive market, online consumer market, the labor market, and the business financing marketplace. This begs the following questions: Where did this tax come from? Has it always been with us? How is it possible that after 400 years, and so much progress, that over 40 million African-Americans only own 2% of American wealth? In Part Two, we'll take a closer look at how we got here but we must first define what we mean by "here." Defined as Black America's current state of affairs, "here" could be characterized in a number of different ways—education, health, business, criminal justice, and politics—but for our purposes, we will look at the economic factors that impact Black Americans' ability to leave a substantial financial legacy for future generations.

A Few Frightening Facts to Consider:

❑ **White households are far wealthier than Black households on every level**
   a) The average (mean) White household has eight times more net worth than the average Black household
   b) The average (mean) wealth of the top 5% of White American households is seven times more than the average of the top 5% of Black households
   c) The average (mean) wealth of the top 1% of White American households is six times more than the average wealth of the top 1% of Black households

❑ **White Americans are significantly more likely to receive an inheritance, and when they do, those inheritances are vastly larger and more likely to increase their wealth profile (the children of baby boomers are about to receive $30 trillion of inheritance over the next several years)**
   a) Whites are five times more likely to get an inheritance than African-Americans
   b) The average White inheritance is 10 times larger than the average African-American inheritance
   c) 91% of the average White inheritance goes to increase wealth vs. just 20% for African-Americans

❑ **White households have far more business equity than Black households**
   a) Wealthy White Americans are four times more likely to have business equity than wealthy African-Americans
   b) Business equity of wealthy White Americans is seven times larger than wealthy African-Americans ($468k vs. $65k)

❑ **White households have a far higher portion of high income earners and far lower portion of households in poverty**
  a) White Americans are overrepresented in almost all high-income occupations and underrepresented in almost all low-income occupations
  b) Black Americans are chronically overrepresented in low-income occupations and significantly underrepresented in almost all high-income occupations

To better understand how African-Americans could own such a small portion of American wealth after being in America *for hundreds of years,* we have to go back to the period of chattel slavery and examine the economic consequences of the anti-Black discriminatory forces that have hindered Black economic development from emancipation to the present day. We'll look at what researchers say about the economic costs that enslaved people, newly freed people, and descendants of enslaved people bore during those times. Those costs, to the extent that they existed, would clearly be a "tax" on Black people and we will use data from various researchers, books, articles, and government statistics to attempt to understand the size, the scope, and the far-reaching ramifications of the tax.

Black Tax From 1619 to 1890–From Slavery to Emancipation

The first 20 or so African captives arrived in Jamestown, Virginia, in 1619. They were originally transported by slave ship from what is modern-day Angola, to Jamestown and forced into slavery. This marked the beginning of slavery as a practice and institution in Colonial America. The slave population in 1619 grew from approximately 20 people to a population of 700,000 slaves by the time of the first U.S. census in 1790, to 2 million in 1830 and then to approximately 4 million by 1860. During that time, America grew from a series of small colonies to a massive independent country that produced the most valuable commodity in the world—raw cotton. Fueled by abundant credit; limitless, cheap fertile land; and an ever-increasing supply of enslaved (free) labor, America became extraordinarily wealthy and powerful and accumulated enough capital to become the greatest beneficiary of the industrial age. The largest appropriation of land that the world has ever seen, combined with the almost complete extinction of tens of millions of indigenous people, augmented by the most brutal and restrictive form of slavery that has ever existed, set the foundation for the greatest accumulation of wealth in the history of the world.

To get a sense of the value of slaves to the American economy, *consider that in 1860 the value of America's 4 million slaves accounted for 16%[27] to 20%[28] of all U.S. wealth or one to two years of national income.* The total U.S. wealth in 2016 was about $85 trillion. The value of slaves as a function of U.S. wealth in 2016 would be the equivalent of $14 trillion to $17 trillion, or about $15.5 trillion. The U.S. national income in 2016 was $19 trillion. The value of slaves as a function of U.S. national income in 2016 would be the equivalent of $19 trillion to $38 trillion or about $28.5 trillion. The average of these estimates is *$22 trillion, which represents the equivalent present value of the future net earnings that those slaves would provide to their masters in 2016.* Today the combined net worth of the more than 40 million African-Americans is currently $1.5 trillion. *This means that 4 million slaves in 1860 had an equivalent economic value that is about 15 times more than the net worth of 40 plus million Black Americans 152 years later.*

Since slavery, by definition, is a 100% tax[29] on all labor produced by a slave, it is imperative that we understand the size of the tax imposed on enslaved people in terms of their uncompensated labor prior to emancipation. *Some researchers have estimated that the value of the labor extracted from enslaved Africans was up to $24 trillion[30] and others up to $97 trillion.[31] Taking an average of these estimates yields a conservative valuation of up to $50 trillion, which is the effective size of tax imposed on Black people between 1619 and 1860.* These estimates do not include any costs associated with the unimaginable pain and suffering (murder, rape, torture, separation of families, denied entrepreneurial enterprise, denial of education, theft of inventions and intellectual property, denial of freedom and the right to pursue happiness) that accompanied the daily life of a slave over the course of 17 generations. *By the way, a trillion is a thousand billion.* So, we are talking about a considerable, almost incalculable sum of money extracted from enslaved Africans that created extraordinary wealth for this country and for White America, that was never recouped by African-Americans.

Black Tax
- Value of slaves in 1860: $22 trillion
- Value of uncompensated labor from 1619 to 1865: up to $50 trillion

---

Black Tax Following Emancipation—40 Acres and a Mule/The Homestead Act

After emancipation, there was some talk about giving recently freed slaves 40 acres of land and a mule. The concept of 40 acres goes back to Special Field Order No. 15 which was issued on Jan. 16, 1865, by Gen. William T. Sherman.[32] If this concept of 40 acres had been extended to all newly freed slaves it would have led to the redistribution of 160 million acres of land to newly freed Black people. At a Republican convention in Pennsylvania, Thaddeus Stevens, a staunch abolitionist, called for the taking of 400 million acres from former slaveholders to provide some compensation and assets to those once enslaved.[33] This land would have allowed former slaves to be able to produce enough goods and services to provide for their basic needs with any surplus allowing for the accumulation of wealth. It would have also provided the former slaves with a modest ability to begin to recover from 17 generations of involuntary and uncompensated servitude. The mule would have provided a means of transportation and the ability to multiply the manual labor of the newly freed people.

It is important to note that by 1860, *80%[34] of the 125,000 craftsmen in the South were slaves, therefore, if the newly freed people had been given land, capital, and access to markets they would have been able to build homes, towns, schools, hospitals, and institutions, but they were not.* Providing 400 million acres to these newly freed people as compensation for unimaginably brutal treatment over 250 years never gained traction and the hope of 40 acres and a mule also never came to fruition. In 1865, Andrew Johnson, President Abraham Lincoln's successor and a supporter of the Southern White supremacist establishment, overturned Special Field Order No. 15 and returned confiscated land to the Southern states and landowners who had committed treason against the United States of America by their staunch support of secession from, and the waging of war against, the United States.

Given the repugnant historical treatment of Black people in America since 1619, this outcome is not surprising. But what is very interesting is that *in 1862, the U.S. Congress passed the Homestead Act, which would distribute 246 million acres over the next 60 years to 1.5 million White families.*[35] The Homestead Act allowed White families to receive up to 160 acres for free if they agreed to work the land and live on it for five years. To put this into perspective, the average cost of an acre in 2015[36] was $3,020 with premium land going for $6,350, which means that *246 million acres would be worth between $740 billion and $1.6 trillion at 2015 land prices, which is the equivalent of giving $500,000 to $1 million per family.* This massive and unprecedented government giveaway helped draw 24 million White immigrants from overpopulated countries in Europe to America, which was seen as a land of enormous opportunity. Of the 1.5 million families that received Homestead land, 99.73% went to White families. Researchers estimate that up to 93 million Americans today are direct beneficiaries of this enormous wealth-generating program.

> **"...during the first eight years after the Homestead Act was passed, over 1 million former slaves got sick or died from exposure and disease."**

Thus, while newly freed people were denied a modest means to produce resources for themselves (after $50 trillion worth of labor had been extracted from themselves and their forbearers), millions of White families, some citizens, many who were not, were given extraordinary opportunity to own valuable land at virtually no cost. The irony is that during the first eight years after the Homestead Act was passed, *over 1 million[37] former slaves got sick or died from exposure and disease*, which Jim Downs, associate professor of history at Connecticut College, describes as the "largest biological crisis of the 19th century." Exposure and disease were the natural outgrowths of insufficient food, clothing, and shelter as a result of former slaves not having land or means to produce resources to sustain themselves. The situation grew so dire that "Nathaniel Shaler, dean of the Lawrence Scientific School at Harvard, suggested in 1884 that Blacks were becoming extinct"[38] and by 1900, the average life expectancy of an African-American child born in that year was just 33 years, whereas a White child's life expectancy was 50% longer.[39]

Black Tax at 2015 Land Prices

- 40 acres—160 million acres or $438 billion to $1 trillion
- 400 million acres proposed by Thaddeus Stevens, or $1.2 trillion to $2.5 trillion
- 246 million acres from the Homestead Act: $740 billion to $1.6 trillion (given to White families, Blacks families excluded)

Black Tax From 1870 to 1935—Jim Crow Society

In 1861, raw cotton accounted for 61% of all U.S. exports. According to Sven Beckert, professor of history at Harvard University, up to 20 million people worldwide were involved in the cultivation of cotton and the production of cotton cloth within the most dynamic and far-reaching production complex in human history.[40] This global cotton production complex relied almost entirely on the free labor from 4 million Black slaves in America, who by 1860 were 80% of the craftsmen in the South and "accounted for approximately 70% of the labor force in the states of South Carolina, Georgia, and Mississippi and upwards of 60% in a number of neighboring states."[41] *Due to the outbreak of the Civil War and the ensuing precipitous drop in cotton production, close to 1 million people lost their cotton-related jobs across Europe and in other nations with cotton industries.*

The resulting devastation of the Civil War and the emancipation of 4 million enslaved Black people left Southern states decimated and the world economy in a global cotton famine. During this cotton famine, a primary concern around the world was how would America put her newly freed people back to work. The answer to that question was the establishment of a system of laws and customs coupled with extreme violence that would reinstitute Southern White supremacist control. This system became known as Jim Crow, and its aim was to reduce newly freed and virtually penniless Black people to a large, cheap, readily available labor force, with no political or economic power. This would be relatively easy to accomplish since, by 1870, newly freed Black Americans owned only about 0.17% of American wealth, and were largely unable to provide for their own basics needs.

The foundation of this new system was a construct called sharecropping. In a sharecropping contract, a White landowner would contract with a Black laborer to plant and harvest cash crops. Since the Black laborer had no land or capital, the White landowner would extend him credit at interest rates often as high as 70%,[42] to buy food for his family, and any tools, seeds, fertilizer, and all other supplies necessary for planting and harvesting the cash crops. In exchange for his work, the Black laborer would be paid based on a "share" of the crops he produced minus any expenses owed to the White landowner. In addition, White landowners would set the terms and the conditions for all aspects of the contract including *(1) the interest rate on the credit that they extended to the Black laborers and (2) the market price for the cash crops that were produced by the Black laborers.* In this way, the White landowner controlled the Black laborer's income (i.e., what he earned on his share of the crops) and his expenses (i.e., the cost of debt and prices of food, materials, and supplies), which meant that the White landowner determined whether or not the Black laborer would have any money left over to provide for himself and his family.

"Landowners, acutely aware that any worker fully clear of his debts might then attempt to relocate to a friendlier or more generous White property holder, routinely exaggerated cost and interest so that virtually no sharecroppers could ever fully extinguish their obligations."[43] If the Black laborer questioned or protested he could face violent and lethal repercussions. As one former sharecropper put it: "I have been living in this Delta 30 years and I know that I have been robbed every year; but there is no use jumping out of the pot into the fire. If we ask questions we are cussed, and if we raise up we are shot and that ends it."[44] This placed the Black laborer in a position where he was unable to accumulate any wealth and was in perpetual debt servitude. The situation was sometimes so draconian, that in many cases, if the Black laborer could not fulfill the terms of the contract, even if it was because he was sick, the White landowner could outsource his work at the Black laborer's expense.

With this immoral and grotesquely unjust sharecropping construct, you would expect the newly freed person to simply not honor the terms of the contract. Unfortunately, Southern authorities passed contract-enforcement laws, which imposed criminal sanctions for the breach of an employment contract. In his book *The Shadow of Slavery* (1972), Pete Daniel wrote: "Under such laws ... a laborer who signed a contract and then abandoned his job could be arrested for a criminal offense. Ultimately the [Black laborer's] choice was simple: he could either work out his contract or go to the state or county chain gang."

You might think an option for the newly freed person could be to simply not enter a sharecropping contract in the first place. The challenge with that is the Black laborer did not have many alternative forms of employment and would end up unemployed, landless, and without a means to feed himself or his family. To ensure that there would always be a cheap supply of Black labor, Southern authorities passed various vagrancy Laws. Alabama's vagrancy law, passed in September

1903, was fairly typical. It defined a vagrant as "any person wandering or strolling about in idleness, who is able to work, and has no property to support him; or any person leading an idle, immoral, profligate life, having no property to support him…"[45] People who were convicted of these vagrancy laws were often sentenced to state or county chain gangs. These vagrancy laws caused many Black laborers to voluntarily attach themselves to White landowners for marginal wages to avoid being convicted and returned to the same farm as uncompensated laborers, in shackles and without their freedom.

To further the exploitation of the Black laborer, many state, county, and local jails in the South engaged in *convict leasing*, which was the practice of leasing out convicts to private firms for profit. This practice, in some respects, was worse than slavery because while "The slaveholder could expect to profit from a slave's future output for his entire working life and thus had an incentive to maintain the slave's health,"[46] the private firm had no such incentive, which led to mortality rates on many of these chain gangs being *as high as 45% a year*. Because convicts had no residual value, leasing them was very profitable for both the private firms and state, county, and local governments. Not only were convicts leased to farms of various sizes, but they were also leased to steel mills, lumber mills, coal mines, and other heavy industries. Many convicts, often malnourished and living in deplorable labor camps, had short life expectancies.

To fill the demand for convicts, Black men were often seized and charged with frivolous crimes, convicted and sent to chain gangs. The practice of seizing Black men was so widespread that "by 1902 the seizure of Black men on the back roads of the South was no longer even a brazen act."[47] The practice became so detestable that Black women who showed up to lumber camps in Southern Alabama, seeking the release of their loved ones, "were simply arrested when they arrived, chained into their cells, and kept to serve the physical desires of the men running the camps. The slave camps and mines produced scores of babies—nearly all of them with White fathers."[48]

To accelerate the time to get a conviction, Southern officials developed the concept of plea bargaining, which "circumvented the 13th Amendment requirement that one be "duly convicted." Governments placed the costs of trial on the accused, and captured Blacks understood that fighting the system meant a longer sentence. Therefore, defendants were expected to "plea bargain" or "confess judgment" in order to lower the costs of the trial... "[T]he South's judicial system had been wholly reconfigured to make one of its primary purposes the coercion of African-Americans to comply with the social customs and labor demands of Whites.[49]

These actions created an abundant supply of convicts in state, county, and local jails, which made it easier for White farmers who would not have had enough capital to own a slave before emancipation to cheaply secure additional labor at a fraction of the cost. The practice was so widespread and profitable that in 1914, 20% of Alabama's state revenue was from convict leasing.[50]

Therefore, the newly freed people (who had no education, no representation in government and no standing in society and were given no land or capital to provide for their basic needs) had to return to the fields as laborers to earn wages. In exchange for his labor, a Black sharecropper often received perpetual debt servitude and extremely limited means to accumulate any resources above his basic needs. If he broke

the contract with the White landowner, he could be convicted of a crime, jailed and forced into labor via convict leasing
under conditions that produced 45% death rates. If he did
not enter into a contract, and could not prove that he was
otherwise gainfully employed, he could be convicted of being
a vagrant or some other petty crime, jailed and returned to
labor via convict leasing under conditions that produced 45%
death rates. It was a ruthlessly efficient system that was the
most effective way to return Black laborers to the fields in
a manner that allowed them to
be "free" in name only.

> **"The devastation was so complete that in 1870 newly freed Black people owned less than 1% of U.S. land and after 147 years, African-Americans still own less than 1% of U.S. land"**

As tragic and heartbreaking
as that system was, its primary
purpose and effect was to impose
a 100% tax on Black labor. By
1910, 93% of African-Americans lived in the South and the
overwhelming majority of them
were subject to a nearly 100%
tax on their labor and by 1935, 40% of the Black labor force
was still engaged in sharecropping, tenant farming or worked
as day laborers. In 1930, there were 1,205,000[51] Black tenants
and day laborers on Southern farms; they were paid an average
income of $71 per year, which was $26 less than White tenants
and day laborers. This difference in compensation cost Black
tenants and day laborers $31 million each year or $157 million
over five years, which is equivalent to $420 million per year or
$2.1 billion over a five-year period in today's dollars.[52]

The period of sharecropping and tenant farming existed
between 1870 and 1945, which was one-third of the length

of state-sponsored chattel slavery in America. Therefore, if one were to assume that *economic value of the resources extracted from Black Americans during this period is a third of the value extracted during the 250-year period of chattel slavery, it would amount to $15 trillion.* In 1860, 4 million slaves were worth the equivalent of $22 trillion, which was wiped out by the Civil War but over the next 75 years, Southern officials were still able to extract that $15 trillion of the $22 trillion they lost, from the descendants of their former slaves, 3.6 million[53] of whom were still working in ultra-low wage jobs in agriculture and domestic service in former slave states 65 years later. The devastation was so complete that in 1870 newly freed Black people owned less than 1% of U.S. land and after 147 years, African-Americans still own less than 1% of U.S. land.

While this Jim Crow period may be hard to imagine, it is important to recall that during this period, (1) the equivalent of one Black American per week was publicly lynched (burned alive, hanged, and mutilated) by their fellow White citizens with no White person ever being convicted of any of these murders. (2) The membership of a White supremacist terrorist organization (the Ku Klux Klan) peaked at 4 million, which meant that up to 25% of the White population had a relative who was a member of this organization. (3) Entire Black towns were destroyed and hundreds of Black Americans were killed by angry White mobs. (4) Black soldiers returning from World War 1 were being lynched in their uniforms by private citizens. And (5) Black citizens had no political representation, almost no means to defend themselves and were severely restricted in almost all labor, capital, service, and educational markets. This was such a violent period for Black Americans who "could be killed for starting a business, accumulating wealth and otherwise trying to improve [their] situation"[54] that between 1910 and 1930 1.6 million Black Americans fled Southern states for Northern U.S. cities and by 1920 a massive "back to Africa" movement had developed, supported by millions of African-Americans.

Black Tax at 2015 prices
• Jim Crow Society: $15 trillion

Black Tax in the Labor Market—Anti-Black Discrimination From 1935 to 1965

In 1934, the median annual income for a White household was about $1,500. For Black households, 65% of whom worked as domestic employees and agricultural workers, the median annual income was $474. As a response to the economic impact of the Great Depression, Congress passed a series of laws to provide economic relief for millions of American citizens. These laws were called the New Deal and helped to set minimum wages, maximum weekly work hours, legalize labor organizing, provide assistance to farmers, and provide old age insurance (Social Security) to senior citizens. The New Deal was a huge undertaking and served as a foundation for the creation of the American middle class. But before the New Deal was passed into law, it was opposed in Congress by representatives from Southern states.

In order to get the New Deal passed into law, two important amendments had to be made to the bill. The first was the exclusion of agricultural and domestic workers from New Deal benefits, and the second would be to allow for the distribution and administration of benefits at the state and local level. Although Black Americans had been relegated to the lowest-wage, lowest-skilled jobs with the least opportunity to accumulate wealth and were in dire need of economic support from the New Deal, the severity of their economic deprivation would continue, because the first amendment to this bill eliminated 65% of the Black labor force and the second change allowed Southern authorities to exclude almost all other Black laborers from getting New Deal benefits. This had far-reaching ramifications:

"In 1935 Congress passed the Wagner Act, which legalized labor organizing but non-Whites were specifically excluded from it. This meant that high-paying union jobs, and the benefits of medical care and job security that went along with them, were denied to non-Whites—an exclusion that lasted well into the 1970s."[55]

"Minimum wage regulations also proved disastrous for Black workers because those regulations made it illegal for employers to hire people who weren't 'worth' the minimum because they lacked skills. As a result, some 500,000 Blacks, particularly in the South, were estimated to have lost their jobs."[56]

"The story in agriculture was particularly grim. Since 40 % of all Black workers made their living as sharecroppers and tenant farmers, the Agricultural Adjustment Administration (AAA) acreage reduction hit Blacks hard. White landlords could make more money by leaving land untilled than by putting land back into production. As a result, the AAA's policies forced more than 100,000 Blacks off the land in 1933 and 1934. Even more galling to Black leaders, the president failed to support an anti-lynching bill and a bill to abolish the poll tax. Roosevelt feared that conservative Southern Democrats, who had seniority in Congress and controlled many committee chairmanships, would block his bills if he tried to fight them on the race question."[57]

The New Deal distributed $50 billion in federal expenditures (from 1933 to 1940[58]) which is the equivalent of almost $570 billion today. *The exclusion of agricultural and domestic workers in the Social Security Act of 1935 would cost Black workers $143 billion in today's[59] dollars. One research study also estimated the cost of labor market discrimination against Black Americans from 1929 to1969 (in 1983 dollars) at $1.6 trillion[60] or $4.4 trillion today (inflated at 3% per annum).*

Black Tax
- Exclusion from the Social Security Act: $143 billion
- Labor market discrimination: $4.4 trillion

Black Tax From the G.I. Bill, 1935 to 1965

The G.I. Bill of Rights was another series of programs that poured an additional $95 billion into expanding opportunities for soldiers returning from World War II. Overall, the G.I. Bill was a dramatic success, and helped a significant portion of the 16 million World War II veterans attend college, receive job training, start businesses, and purchase their first homes.[61] However, less than 2% of those funds went to the 1 million Black soldiers returning from World War II.

Because of highly discriminatory policies and practices, Black veterans were essentially unable to purchase homes. This was true both in the North and in the South. "In the New York metropolitan area, in 1950, for example, only about 69 of 69,666 VA loans, less than one-tenth of one percent, were held by non-Whites"[62] and in Mississippi, in 1947, only two out of 3,229 VA loans went to Black veterans.

Job training was also very difficult for returning Black soldiers to get. "By October 1946, 6,500 former soldiers had been placed in nonfarm jobs by the employment service in Mississippi; of those jobs, 86% of the skilled and semiskilled jobs were filled by Whites, 92% of the unskilled ones by Blacks."[63]

Discrimination was also a key factor in limiting Black soldiers' ability to get post-secondary educational opportunities. Elite Northern colleges enrolled almost no Black students in the late 1940s. Take for example, the University of Pennsylvania and Columbia, which were among the least discriminatory of the Ivy League colleges, yet still enrolled only 46 Black students even though they had combined student bodies of 9,000 in 1946.[64]

Because Blacks were excluded from White schools in the North and still under segregation in the South, approximately 95% of Black veterans had to seek post-secondary education at the 100 Black colleges in the South that were chronically underfunded and lacking first-rate facilities. While White universities were expanding to accommodate millions of White veterans, Black colleges did not have, and were not given, the resources to accommodate an estimated 70,000 Black veterans in 1947. One report showed that as much as 55% of Black veterans who applied to Black colleges for post-secondary education were turned away because they could not accommodate the demand. *The federal government invested $95 billion via the G.I. Bill to create opportunities for returning soldiers, which is equivalent to $700 billion today, yet less than 2% of the money went to Black veterans. And while less than 2% of Black Americans had a college degree by 1950, and Blacks in general had a strong desire and need for post-secondary education, they would be kept out of colleges and universities for another 20 years while millions of Whites received government subsidies for post-secondary education.*

Black Tax
- G.I. Bill: Up to $45 billion denied to Black Soldiers

Black Tax—Separate But Equal Education From 1896 to 1954

After emancipation, former slaves clamored for access to educational opportunities. They demanded, and succeeded in helping to institute, a public school system in the South that had not existed before. These gains were jeopardized after 1867, when the planter class (i.e., wealthy White former slave owners) came back to power and wanted to halt the expansion of universal education to Southern children because they did not want to pay for it. They also wanted a vast amount of unskilled Black laborers to work in the fields to drive profits for their operations. These unskilled laborers would also not be educated enough to challenge Whites' absolute control of politics and creation of policy and regulations. However, White farmers with smaller farms also wanted continued expansion of public education for their children and the White planter class needed their support. The White planters and farmers ultimately decided to support and expand universal education, with public school funds for Black children being diverted to White children with both the planter class and White small farm owners increasing their opposition to Black education. This opposition had been so effective in limiting investment in Black education in the South during the 40 years since the Civil War, that in 1903 W.E.B. Du Bois, in his influential essay *The Talented Tenth*, stated that "negro taxes and the negro's share of income from indirect taxes and endowments have fully repaid this expenditure [i.e., Southern White investment in negro education since the Civil War]."

The Separate but Equal doctrine established by the Supreme Court in 1896 (which stated that separate but equal facilities for Black and White Americans did not violate the "equal protection under the law" provision in the 14th amendment of the U.S. Constitution) not only upheld racial segregation but also proved to be the perfect vehicle for the planter class and the White farmers to legally divert funding away from Black students to White students. This diverting of resources was so pervasive that by 1900, there were only about 27,000 Black teachers for the 2.5 million Black children aged 5 to 18 in the former 16 slave states, and of the 2.1 million Black children aged 5 to 14 only 36% were attending school. According to Eugene Kinckle Jones, one of the founding members of the nation's first Black fraternity (Alpha Phi Alpha Fraternity, Inc.), in 1920 South Carolina's segregated school system spent $1.25[65] per Black student compared to the $66 per student spent in the New York City school system. In 1920, New York City, which had a population that was almost entirely White (97.1%),[66] spent over 50 times more per child on education than South Carolina spent on each Black child in its segregated system, even though Blacks were 51.4%[67] of the State's population.

Between 1900 and 1920, despite significant tax increases to build schools in the South, virtually none of that money was used for Black schools. By 1917, there were only 64 public high schools for Black students across the entire South. In 1909, Richard Wright, one of the foremost African-American educators of the post-Reconstruction era, found that 44% of school buildings used to educate Black children in 155 districts across 11 former slaves states were privately owned by Blacks. "Moreover, [Wright] discovered that many schoolhouses reported as public domains were paid for in large part by Blacks through voluntary contributions."[68] Therefore, to "have their privately financed schools recognized and even partially supported by state or local school authorities, Black Southerners had to deed to the state their contributions of money, land and school equipment."[69] This

> "The fundamental problem with the idea of separate but equal was that it was impossible to make facilities equal in a culture and society that was based on almost 300 years of pervasive, coercive, and systematic inequality and inequity."

led to a double taxation on Blacks, who while having less than 1% of all U.S. wealth, and often comprised 30% to 60% of many Southern school districts, were forced to subsidize White communities, which combined, controlled 99% of the U.S. wealth.

The fundamental problem with the idea of separate but equal was that it was impossible to make facilities equal in a culture and society that was based on almost 300 years of pervasive, coercive, and systematic inequality and inequity. The terrifying result of this doctrine was that it provided a legal vehicle for Southern states to continue to invest as little as possible in the education of Black children over the course of six generations between 1865 and when the law was found to be unconstitutional in 1954.

In many cases:
 a) Black teachers in the South were paid only 25% to 34% of what White teachers were paid (White teachers made up to 300% more than Black teachers)
 b) Between $5 to $8[70] were invested to educate a White child, for every dollar invested to educate a Black student (White students received up to 700% more than Black students)
 c) White students also received 50% more years of education than Blacks by age 25
 d) White students were four times more likely to complete high school and almost five[71] times more likely to complete college than Black students

Education was also problematic at the post-secondary level, with Blacks excluded from White universities in the South and almost all universities in the North along with many Black universities and colleges in the South being chronically underfunded. In 1914, William H. Baldwin, the president of the

General Education Board whose "objective was the promotion of education within the United States of America, without distinction of race, sex or creed" stated that "the South needed negroes educated so that they could be directed to be the best possible laborers. With the right kind of education, the negro will willingly work menial jobs, and that would open up an opportunity for Southern Whites to perform more expert labor.[72] "A mere 50 years earlier, Blacks were 80% of all craftsmen in the South and now they were being educated to "work menial jobs." During Jim Crow, most high-skilled trades and jobs were reserved for White Americans, and caused the percentage of Black craftsmen to plummet to minuscule levels. This is entirely consistent with the experience of millions of Black people in the South and has compounded the Black tax exponentially up to present day.

The overall effect of this "objective" was so far-reaching that researchers estimate that a truly "separate but equal" school system would have reduced wage inequality between Black and White workers by up to 50%. Think about it this way: If all of the other discrimination in society, politics, and the labor market stayed the same, the power of an equal education could have reduced the wage gap by up to 50%,[73] if Black students were given equal resources and opportunities. We're talking about generations of Black workers whose earning power was severely reduced. *"This reduced earning power could have amounted to $1 billion in 1940 alone or up to $42 billion in today's dollars (if inflated between 3–5%). The impact on one generation could have been up to $635 billion. And the impact on the six generations of Black children between emancipation (1865) and when separate but equal was found to be unconstitutional in 1954 could be up to $3 trillion in today's dollars."*

Black Tax From Desegregation— What Happened To Black Teachers?

Separate but equal officially lasted from 1896 to 1954 when it was overturned by the Brown v. Board of Education decision. While this was a great victory in general, there were some unintended and devastating consequences to Black students, teachers, and administrators. There was a dramatic reduction in the number of Black teachers at all levels. In 1954, about 82,000 Black teachers were responsible for teaching 2 million Black children and represented approximately 50%[74] of the Black professional class. *In the decade following the Brown decision, almost 40,000 Black teachers[75] and administrators in 17 Southern and border states lost their jobs.* Black teachers were eliminated and ultimately replaced with a pipeline of White teachers.

In Arkansas, virtually no Black educators were hired in desegregated districts in the decade between 1958 to 1968. In Texas, 5,000 "substandard" White teachers were employed, while certified Black teachers "were told to go into other lines of work," says Carol Karpinski, an independent researcher and New York City educator. During that time, Black teachers received little help from unions. According to Helen Pate

Bain, the National Education Association's (NEA's) president from 1970–71, the American Teachers Association (an all-Black union) was too weak, and the larger NEA "was controlled by prejudiced people" in the mid-1950s. *Black principals were in a far worse position. Researchers estimate that 90% of Black principals lost their jobs across 11 Southern states.* In North Carolina, for example, the number of Black principals decreased from 620 to 40 in the four-year period between 1967 to 1971.

Children often choose careers that they encounter from family and social networks. Mildred Hudson, chief executive officer of education management company Recruiting New Teachers, observed that between 1975 to 1985, the number of Black students majoring in education dropped by 66%. This precipitous drop in Black teachers clearly had a significant effect on the networks and the career paths that Black children were exposed to and would ultimately choose from. By the year 2000, 84% of the nation's teachers were White, while only 61% of students were White and *38% of public schools did not have a single teacher of color.* Blacks make up about 18% of public school students but fewer than 8% of teachers and Black males represent less than 2% of all teachers and administrators in the U.S. education system. Findings from the National Center for Education Statistics indicate that in 2011 there were 3.2 million teachers and 49.4 million students in Pre-K to 12th grade. *Black teachers are 7% of total U.S. teachers while Black students were 18% of the students, which means that there should be 352,000 more Black teachers in the country. Since the average U.S. teacher makes $46,953,[76] the cost of these missing Black teachers is $16.5 billion per year (or over $20 billion per year including salary and benefits) for the Black community in the States.*

This dramatic reduction in Black teachers lead to an increase in Black children being taught by White teachers who had both conscious and unconscious bias against them. Consider the results of several studies discussed in *Teacher Education Quarterly* in the winter of 2002.

> "Gottlieb (1964) discovered wide disparities in the use of adjectives to describe the actions of Black students by a set of Black and White teachers, with the positive adjectives attributed to Black teachers. A questionnaire designed by Griffin and London (1979) revealed a majority of the Black teachers polled believed their students possessed adequate or better ability for school success.
>
> White teachers in the same study viewed a majority of the Black students below minimum levels of ability for achievement. Finally, Beady and Hansell (1981) discovered Black teachers held substantially higher expectations for college success for Black students than White teachers did."[77]

From 1865 to 1955, six generations of Black children experienced severe underfunding in the U.S. education system, which effectively crippled their human capital development and reduced their earning capacity by 50%. Yet, despite severe underfunding, they were educated by Black teachers who identified with them, and had high expectations and even higher requirements. Here is a description of the commitment and impact that a Black teacher in 1940s Pine Bluff, Arkansas, had on Ivory Perry, a civil right activist who fought against poverty and lead poisoning in the Black community in St Louis...

> "What he learned at home found powerful reinforcement at school, especially in the classes of Miss Myrtle Jones, his 10th grade teacher at Pine Bluff's Merrill High

School. By the time Ivory entered her class, Miss Jones had already established her identity as an indispensable resource and role model for Black children in the areas ... Before students could enter her classroom, Miss Jones held inspection to make sure that they had combed their hair, cleaned their fingernails, and shined their shoes ... she wanted them armed with respect for themselves and respect for others ... Black educators like Miss Jones had the difficult task of encouraging their students for success in a society that had stacked the deck against them ... Miss Jones asked her students to look deeply inside themselves for the internal resources to transcend their unfair, unjust and immoral circumstances ... self-discipline constituted the core of her philosophy. She took an active role in policing the extracurricular activities of her pupils, driving up and down Pine Bluff's notorious Third Avenue in her big white Chevrolet ... all she had to do was honk her horn at her students and they would dutifully turn around, go home, tell their parents, and accept their punishment ... when she retired from teaching ... she continued youth work for 20 years ... after retiring from that job she continued to do the same work on her own without pay ... It was important to her that young people do something for others and that they recognized their responsibility to society..." [78]

After the Brown v. Board of Education decision, Black students transitioned to a system that had more funding, but eliminated tens of thousands of Black teachers, and increased their exposure to teachers with negative biases and decreased expectations. This was a net loss to the Black community because Black teachers, principals and administrators were replaced with White teachers, principals, and administrators. This diverted tens of billions of dollars of incremental funding away from the Black community (via firing of Black teachers) and shifted it to the White community via the hiring of White teachers.

> **BLACK TAX**
> - Elimination of 25% of Black professional class
>
> - Elimination of a pipeline that would produce generations of Black teachers and administrators
>
> - Black children exposed to higher concentration of teachers with lower expectations and anti-Black biases
>
> - 352,000 fewer Black teachers and $20 billion per year of income and benefits missing from Black families
>
> - Up to $1 trillion of teacher salaries and benefits missing from Black families since 1954

Black Tax From Housing Discrimination, 1935 to 1965

Between 1934 and 1962 the federal government provided over $120B in federal homeowner subsidies to American households. *This was an enormous investment (equivalent to $1 trillion today) which had a direct hand in creating the American middle class and fostering the growth of suburban neighborhoods.* While less than 2% of this money went to African-American families, 20 million White European immigrants and their descendants benefited heavily from these programs. This investment allowed White homeowners to build enormous wealth that could then be used to fund college educations and home improvements; start a business; or put toward an inheritance. Qualified Black borrowers were prevented from accessing these resources and were effectively barred from living in White communities that benefited from this unprecedented level of government support and home price appreciation. The irony is that tax dollars from Black households were used to subsidize this discrimination against them.

Below is an example of the phalanx of opposition that qualified Black buyers faced.

a) Federal Government—Through redlining, the Federal Housing Administration (FHA) refused to provide financing in neighborhoods where Blacks lived to Blacks who wanted to buy homes in White neighborhoods and to developers who did not "maintain neighborhood stability via racial segregation"[79]

b) Business Sector—Andrew Wiese, in his 2004 book *Places of Their Own: African American Suburbanization in the Twentieth Century*, noted that White financial institutions almost uniformly refused to lend money to African-Americans to buy property outside "established Negro areas"

c) Business Sector—According to Wiese, "White real-estate agents refused to be a part of transactions that permitted Blacks to move into White neighborhoods"

d) Residential Sector—White home builders refused to sell or rent homes to African-Americans and other minorities. "Between 1946 and 1960, over 350,000 homes were constructed with FHA financing in Northern California, of which fewer than 100 went to African-Americans"[80]

e) Private Individuals—Whites formed neighborhood associations where homeowners signed race-restrictive covenants, which prohibited the sale or rental of property to "other than Caucasians"

The results of these actions were that between 1930 and 1960, less than 1%[81] of all mortgages in the nation were issued to Black Americans. "Overall, by 1972 nearly 11 million families had entered the ranks of homeownership with the assistance of the FHA and an additional 22 million families were able to make improvements to their homes."[82] And less than 2% of this discriminatory and segregationist-based financial support went to African-Americans.

Below is an excerpt from a 2015 *Time* magazine article about how difficult it was for even a national baseball hero like Jackie Robinson to purchase a home in the New York metropolitan area.

"The Robinsons attempted to buy land in New Canaan but were rebuffed. Rachel called about one house in Greenwich and, after giving her name, the owners refused to show it. The couple settled for a property just across the state line in New York. Jackie recalled that in autumn 1953, "we finally found a piece of land in New York's Westchester County that was just what we wanted." The Robinsons offered the asking price, waited for weeks, and were told that the price would be raised by $5,000. This was standard practice in housing discrimination, a surefire way for Whites in exclusive towns to claim that they had nothing against African-Americans—it was just that Blacks could not meet the asking price. This was purely the market at work, they would say, not racism. So, the Robinsons promptly kicked in the extra $5,000. "There was another period of confused silence," Jackie recalled. "At last, we were told that the land had been sold to somebody else. It was this way everywhere we went." Suburban Whites did not want an African-American for a neighbor, even if it was Jackie Robinson. After the *Bridgeport Herald* printed an article about the Robinsons' experience, the citizens of North Stamford, Connecticut, were moved to action. Ministers circulated non-discrimination petitions. The Robinsons finally bought a home on Cascade Road."[83]

Jackie Robinson was a baseball superstar, a veteran, a military officer, and an American hero and White homeowners refused to allow him and his wife to purchase several homes, which they could afford. It took a concerted effort for the Robinsons to be able to buy their home in North Stamford. So, you can imagine how truly difficult it was for ordinary Black Americans of any class, stature, or income level to do the same.

Between 1940 and 1970, 3.6 million[84] Black Americans fled the economic hardships of the South to cities in the North and faced far greater difficulties than Rachel and Jackie Robinson, because they were effectively barred by discrimination from government policy, private business and neighborhood residents from acquiring property in White neighborhoods and were forced into concentrated areas of poverty and economic deprivation.

Because less than 1% of all mortgages across the nation went to African-Americans, many Black homebuyers often had no choice but to enter into predatory lending contracts called contract sales. In a contract sale, appraisals were not needed to finance the transactions, so the property was often given extreme markups in price, *sometimes up to twice the market value*. Because it was a private contract, usury laws and interest ceilings did not apply so sellers charged extremely high interest rates. To make matters worse, the terms on the contract sale allowed the seller to keep the deed, which prevented the buyer from earning any ownership interest in the home while he was making payments.

If a buyer missed a single payment, he would forfeit the entire down payment, all monthly payments made up to that point, and lose the property. This practice was so extensive, that one leading advocate from the 1950s estimated that 85%[85] of the properties purchased by African-Americans in Chicago were sold via contract sales. Instead of participating in government programs that created trillions of dollars in wealth for the fellow White citizens, Blacks were confined to high-poverty neighborhoods, excluded from buying property in high-appreciating White neighborhoods and charged extremely inflated prices and predatory interest rates while trying to pursue the American Dream.

Because less than 1% of all mortgages across the nation went to African -Americans, many Black homebuyers often had no choice but to enter into predatory lending contracts called contract sales.

The highly discriminatory environment in the workforce, and the virtual exclusion of Blacks from the equivalent of trillions of dollars of government subsidies had an extremely negative impact on the ability of Black Americans to accumulate wealth. *By 1950, White Americans had accumulated 150[86] times more capital than Black Americans, which made it easier for them to buy homes, start businesses, and fund college educations for their children. White Americans born between 1943 and 1951 would also go on to accumulate an average wealth of $1.2 million[87] by 2013 which is 11 times more wealth than Black Americans born in the same period.* These government benefits went to the parents of the White baby boomer generation who were then able to leave trillions of dollars of inheritance to the baby boomer generation, who will now leave over $30 trillion[88] of inheritance to their children over the next several decades ($4.2 trillion of which would have been an inheritance from Black baby boomer families to their children, if not for overwhelming and near universal presence of anti-Black discrimination).

Black Tax
- Blacks received almost none of the $1 trillion government subsidies
- $4.2 trillion of inheritance is missing from the children of Black baby boomers
- $4.8 trillion of missing African-American primary home equity

---

Black Tax From 1965 to the Present

Despite the monumental efforts of the Civil Rights Movement, which created massive opportunities for Black Americans to (1) attend world-class universities, (2) pursue exciting and lucrative occupations and career paths, (3) start new businesses, and (4) gain access to capital and government contracts, studies have shown that there has been little change in the relative rank in the overall earnings distribution of Black and White men since 1940. In 1940, the median Black wage earner made less than 75%[89] of all White wage earners, while in 2009 the median Black wage earner made less than 73% of all White wage earners.

Gains from the Civil Rights Movement can easily be seen

in the Black students who gained access to numerous predominantly White universities, went on to work for major companies and attained important leadership roles throughout Corporate America. This allowed Black men in the 90th percentile of Black wage earners to close some of the earnings gap with their White peers. In 1940, Black 90th-percentile wage earners made as much money as White 50th-percentile wage earners, but by 2014 Black 90th-percentile wage earners made as much as White 75th-percentile wage earners. While these 90th-percentile wage earners never achieved parity with their White peers, many of them were able to move out of economically depressed areas into communities with the resources and opportunities to prepare their children to succeed at the highest levels, despite facing significant discrimination. Their accomplishments were extraordinary given the pervasive effects of racial discrimination in the workplace, which *researchers estimate cost about $94 billion to $123[90] billion in 1970 alone.*

While Blacks in the 90th percentile did relatively well, Black men in the 75th percentile saw their earnings stagnate and Black men at the 50th percentile saw their earnings decline by 32%. This decline was driven by a dramatic increase in the percentage of Black men of prime working age (24 to 55) with zero earnings (i.e., no income) which almost doubled from 17% in 1970 to 35%[91] in 2014. This dramatic increase was driven by:

(1) Globalization—the movement of manufacturing jobs (especially low-skilled jobs) from U.S. inner cities to low-cost jurisdictions (i.e., low-wage countries) around the world. From 1940 to 1970, approximately 3.4 million African-Americans left the South to escape violence and disenfranchisement and to secure manufacturing jobs in Northern cities. By 1970,

70%[92] of all African-Americans working in metro areas had blue-collar jobs and as the manufacturing jobs disappeared, so did the "secondary employment opportunities (e.g., those in stores, support services and banks)"[93] and millions of Black families fell into poverty.

(2) An increased premium on high-skilled jobs requiring a college education or specialized training and a decreased value placed on low-wage jobs.

(3) White Americans' reactions to the perceived advancement of Black Americans due to civil rights.

   a) Mass incarceration stemming from "tough on crime," "law and order," "the war on drugs," "mandatory minimum sentences," and other criminal justice policies that devastated the Black community.

   b) Reduced tax base and property values driven by continued "White flight" out of inner cities into surrounding suburbs with little to no Black presence.

(4) The continued presence of anti-Black discrimination in the workplace

Because Black Americans have been historically forced to occupy the lowest-wage, lowest-skilled positions in the workforce, they were disproportionately affected by the movement of low-wage jobs overseas. Even though Black American educational attainment increased rapidly between 1940 and 2010 it was not sufficient to offset the shift away from low-skilled jobs. In 1940, about 7% of Black Americans had completed high school and by 2010 almost 90%[94] had completed high school. While this is impressive, the value of a high school education fell dramatically after the 1970s. This meant that *Black Americans rapidly attained a degree that prepared them for low-skilled manufacturing jobs that were rapidly disappearing from inner cities*. Therefore, the movement of jobs away from the inner cities and the limited employment opportunities remaining for low-skilled labor, led to increased unemployment, depression, and crime in Black neighborhoods.

In 1940, about 1.6% of Black Americans had completed college and by 1970 that number had increased to about 5%.[95] The few Black Americans who were able to receive specialized training or attend colleges, were able to capture some of the increased premium what was being placed on higher-skilled occupations. However, desegregation, various race riots during the late 1960s coupled with White American conscious and unconscious bias against Black Americans, led many Whites to fear an increase in crime and a decrease in property values as Black Americans gained more ability to move into neighborhoods from which they had been previously excluded. This made many Whites move out of inner cities and into suburban areas where there were fewer African-Americans. As some Black Americans also began to move into suburban areas, White Americans moved even further out to the outer suburbs where there were fewer Blacks. As White Americans left inner cities and inner suburbs they took the wealth and capital with them and this "White flight" combined with the job losses from globalization, further depressed property values and significantly reduced the tax base that many urban areas needed to fund public education and fire and safety departments. This reduction in tax base weakened public education in inner cities where most Black Americans now lived.

"33% of Black men born in 2001 are expected to be incarcerated in their lifetimes and will be likely unable to vote and find employment due to background checks."

The resulting lack of economic opportunities in Black neighborhoods increased the appeal of illegal drugs both as an escape for users and as a means of economic advancement for low-level sellers. The continued fear of Black Americans bringing crime to previously White neighborhoods also led to a rash of legislation that increased policing in Black neighborhoods, increased the length and severity of sentences for various crimes, and treated drug use, and selling of drugs at the street level as a criminal justice issue instead of a health-care and economic problem. The consequence had a devastating effect on Black men and a long-lasting impact on Black households.

a) The percent of incarcerated Black men increased from 2% in 1970 to 8% in 2014

b) The percent of out-of-work Black men increased from 8% in 1970 to 16% in 2014

c) The percent of Black men not working but looking for employment increased from 7% in 1970 to 11% in 2014

This Black tax led to the percentage of Black men of prime working age (24 to 55) earning zero income, increasing from 17% in 1970 to 35% in 2014. The impact became so dire, that as of 2001, 2,166,000 African-Americans had been imprisoned or 9.2% of the African-American population over the age of 18. In addition, 33% of Black men born in 2001 are expected to be incarcerated in their lifetimes and will be likely unable to vote and find employment due to background checks. Today, African-Americans constitute nearly 1 million of the total 2.3 million people incarcerated costing $30.4 billion per year. If those men were out of jail and earning

$15 per hour, collectively, they would add $30 billion per year to their family's income and lift millions of Black children out of poverty. In 1970,[96] nearly 70% of Black families were composed of married couples, by 1990 the removal of young Black men from mass incarceration had lowered the percentage of Black households composed of married couples to less than 50%. *Today Black families are losing $30 billion per year and American society is losing $60 billion per year because of the 1 million Black men in jail. The $30 billion spent incarcerating 1 million Black men could cover the cost of a public college education and technical vocational training for all of these men.*

The culmination of centuries of the Black tax has also left African-Americans with not only a disproportionate share of low-paying jobs but also with an unemployment rate that has been twice that of White Americans since 1960, which is almost 60 years. This means that as of 2010, if Blacks had the same employment rate as White Americans, an additional 2 million African-Americans would have been employed, which amounts to almost $80 billion per year of lost income and benefits to the Black community or $3.3 trillion over the last six decades.

Black Tax From 1619 to the Present —A Short Summary

Over $70 trillion of resources were extracted from and/or not provided to African-Americans, which effectively destroyed Black America's ability to accumulate wealth and leave a substantial legacy for our children's children. Let's take a look at the numbers; they are a frightening and sobering look at how pervasive and systematic discrimination and biases have taxed and negatively affected Black America.

a)	**Slavery (1619 to 1865)**	$50 trillion
b)	**Present value of Black labor in 1860**	$22 trillion
c)	**Homestead Act (1862 to 1935)**	$1.6 trillion
d)	**Sharecropping/Jim Crow Society (1870 to 1935)**	$15 trillion

e) Great economic expansion 1935 to 1965

	Labor	$4.4 trillion
❑	Education	$2 trillion
❑	Housing	$1.75 trillion

f) Post-Civil Rights era (1960 to the present)

❑	Six decades of a persistent Black/White employment gap	$3.3 trillion
❑	Missing intergenerational inheritance	$4.2 trillion

g) Continuing costs

- ❑ $317 billion per year—current cost of lost equity value
- ❑ $20 billion per year—current cost of 350,000 missing Black teachers
- ❑ $30 billion per year—current lost income from Black prison population
- ❑ $80 billion per year—persistent six-decade Black/White employment gap
- ❑ $72 billion to $93 billion lost in 2005 to foreclosures from discriminatory subprime lending
- ❑ $94 billion to $123 billion—cost of workplace discrimination in 1970

Decades of a discriminatory Black tax effectively excluded Black Americans from receiving trillions of dollars of government support that was invested in the economic development of White families, communities, businesses, and institutions. While these anti-Black discriminatory practices (executed by both the government, private citizens, and institutions) allowed White families to buy homes, fund college education, start new businesses, and participate in almost 80 years of unprecedented stock and real estate market appreciation, Black Americans, when not subjected to mass incarceration, were largely confined to neighborhoods with intergenerational poverty, high unemployment, substandard education, and economic deprivation.

Despite this massive historical Black tax, and the tens of billions of dollars of Black tax associated with implicit and explicit bias in the real-estate, automotive and business financing markets, the mass incarceration of Black men, and the discrimination in the workforce, *the perception held by most White Americans is that Black Americans don't try hard enough.* Consider the following polling data:

a) The prevailing view among almost 70% of Whites is that Blacks use racism as an excuse for failure[97]

b) 63% of Americans believe that Blacks not trying hard enough is more to blame for their not getting ahead than any racial discrimination[98] —The Pew Research Center for the People and the Press, January 2012

c) 61% of Whites believe that Blacks have equal opportunities with Whites[99]

While these views seem comical, unbelievable, and down-right frustrating in light of the massive costs that have been imposed on Black Americans and the funds invested in White Americans, they are still held by millions of Americans and play a large role in the formulation and execution of policies that affect Black American wealth accumulation and economic development. ✪

It must be considered that there is nothing more difficult to carry out, no more doubtful of success, nor more dangerous to handle, than to initiate a new order of things.
— The Prince, Niccolò Machiavelli

PART THREE

WHAT CAN WE DO ABOUT THE BLACK TAX?

Where Are We Now?

For any people to thrive, their society must be built on a foundation of seven pillars. Those pillars are Opportunity, Trade, Industry and Innovation, Capital, Skill and Security, which form the acronym OPTICS. Trade is the ability to exchange goods and services for economic benefit and Industry is the process of producing goods and services for trade. Innovation is the utilization of technology to improve things of value. Capital is the financial means to develop the infrastructure to make goods and trade them. Skill is the ability to do something that others cannot, or to do it substantially better than others can. Security is the state of being able to retain and maintain your life, liberty, and property. Opportunity is the ability to participate in a valuable endeavor. Trade, Industry and Innovation, Capital, Skill and Security all require Opportunity. Every great nation, past and present, has been built on the seven pillars of OPTICS. The Black tax has devastated the OPTICS for Black Americans, leaving us with just 2% of American wealth while we struggle within a 2% paradigm (or rule) that seems to emerge again and again in areas of vital importance to African-American economic development.

This 2% rule is driven by the massive and continuous level of anti-Black discrimination and disenfranchisement that served as a confiscatory tax on Black people's ability to accumulate wealth. Chattel slavery in America was a 250-year period of a 100% tax on enslaved people, which stripped the ancestors of Black Americans of $50 trillion, and left newly emancipated people owning approximately 0.17% of American wealth after emancipation. This was followed by a 100-year nightmare from emancipation through Jim Crow to the end of the Civil Rights Movement, where Black Americans faced another massive confiscatory tax on Opportunity, Trade, Industry and Innovation, Capital, Skill and Security. Within each of these pillars, Black Americans received the lowest level of investment and the highest level of restrictions. This created a great appreciation among African-Americans for any form of advancement, accomplishment, or attainment above the absolute minimum allowed by White Americans, and made the 2% phenomena I outline below, tolerable for an entire people. The combined 350-year period of slavery and Jim Crow apartheid, was then followed by 50 years of extraordinary progress for the top 10% of African-American families and a massive amount of economic deprivation, mass incarceration, and intergenerational poverty for millions of others.

The 2% Rule

R esearch shows that Black Americans were often re-stricted to 2% levels or less in many vitally import-ant aspects of the economy, politics, and society at large, that facilitated wealth accumulation.

Black Americans:

- Were emancipated but denied land, capital, credit, fair wages, means of production, skills development and free trade (all of which were far below the 2% level)

- Held less than 2% of U.S. wealth for 350 years

- Owned less than 2% of all U.S. land for 400 years (currently 1%)

- Held less than 2% of almost all high-skilled, high-paying jobs in all industries for 150 years after emancipation

- Received less than 2% of 246 million acres distributed to 1.5 million American families (actually less than 0.27%)

- Received less than 2% of the $120 billion distributed to Americans via federal housing subsidies

- Received less than 2% of the $95 billion distributed to Americans via the G.I. Bill

- Received less than 2% of the $50 billion distributed to Americans via the New Deal

- Received less than 2% of agriculture subsidy payments distributed to American farmers

- Less than 2% of the adult Black population was allowed to attain college degrees as of 1950

Today, Black Americans have unknowingly settled into a 2% equilibrium with their most vital financial enterprises. Black Americans:

- Spend less than 2% of their combined $1.2 trillion income on Black enterprises

- Deposit less than 2% of their combined $130 billion of deposits in Black banks

- Spend less than 2% of their combined $1.2 trillion income on education

This has a massive depressive impact on job creation, business development and business formation. It seems that what was done to Black Americans by their fellow citizens, Black Americans now do within their own communities and to Black enterprises and businesses. This minuscule level of commercial activity with Black enterprises starves Black businesses of capital, dramatically reduces demand for their goods and services, limits the development of an industrial base with economies of scale, and further depresses the demand for additional employment and skill development at all levels within the Black community. All of which helps to (1) prevent the community from being comprised of a healthier mix of producers and consumers and (2) keeps it comprised almost exclusively of low-income consumers.

This low level of investment and economic engagement in Black enterprises by African-Americans serves as an additional tax, which further stifles job creation and wealth accumulation in our communities. Because of this, Black Americans are faced with two Black taxes, one imposed by their fellow citizens and one imposed by themselves. Whether driven by conscious or unconscious bias, Black Americans spend an extraordinarily small amount of their income and deposit a similarly small amount of capital in their own banks. The net effect of these actions is highly discriminatory in nature and impact. Gary Becker, in his book The Economics of Discrimination (1957), wrote that discrimination lowers the incomes of both the party that discriminates, and the party that is discriminated against. This second form of the Black tax, driven by Black Americans discriminating against themselves, has the doubly negative effect of lowering the incomes for both Black enterprises and the Black consumers. It is also important to note that the less capital each party has, the larger the effect discrimination has on lowering each party's income. Since Black enterprises and Black consumers have very little capital, the discriminatory effect has an even greater impact on reducing income within the community.

Unfortunately, many companies and institutions have also settled into a mode of investing 2% or less in Black people and Black enterprises. Their actions seem to convey an unwillingness or disinterest in investing more in Black employment and Black enterprises than Black Americans are willing to invest in and demand for themselves.

Consider the following list of instances where the 2% rule is still in effect today:

Investment and Business Financing

- Black-owned small businesses received less than 2% (1.7%) of all loan money distributed through the SBA, according to an analysis by the Wall Street Journal

- Less than 2% (1.5%) of total corporate procurement dollars are spent with Black-owned businesses—2014 Corporate Diversity Survey

- Less than 2% (1%) of tech companies with Black founders receive venture capital funding— FastCoexist.com

- Research conducted by Venrock Vice President Richard Kerby in 2015 found that Black investors comprised less than 2% (1.7%) of the venture capital industry

Corporate Leadership

- Less than 2% (1%) of Fortune 500 CEOs are Black (source: AOL.Com Finance)

- Less than 2% (1.9%) of partners at law firms are African-American (source: the American Lawyer's Diversity Scorecard)

- African-Americans only account for 2.7% of senior-level staff in the financial industry (source: motherjones.com)

- Black employees comprise 2% of investment professionals (source: Venture Capital Firms)

- Blacks only make up about 2% of recent hires at tech firms (source: The Atlantic magazine)

Education

- Less than 2% of school teachers and administrators nationwide are Black men

- Less than 2% of the nation's 3,000 colleges and universities' tenured faculty are Black

- In 2004, Blacks earned less than 2% of doctorates in Math, Physics and Computer Science and all Engineering disciplines

- HBCUs received less than 2% of the more than $140 billion in federal grants for science and engineering awarded in the 1990s

Media

- Blacks consume more media per person than any other group, yet...

- Less than 2% (1%) of film executives and directors who are members of the Academy of Motion Picture Arts and Sciences are Black

- Less than 2% of advertising expenditures ($70B—Cable TV, national magazines, network TV, spot radio, syndicated TV) goes to Black media outlets

Medicine and Law

- Black women make up 2% of all doctors in the United States yet...

- Black women make up less than 2% of all lawyers in the United States

- Black men make up 2% of all doctors in the United States

- Black men make up less than 2% of all lawyers in the United States

Financial Services

- Blacks spend $150B per year financing cars and homes

- Blacks make up 1% to 2% of all financial advisors, according to industry executives interviewed by FinancialPlanning.com

- Finance and insurance businesses account for just 2.2% of all African-American businesses, according to the most recent statistics from the U.S. Department of Commerce

Agriculture

- Black Americans currently own less than 2% (.9%) of U.S. land, which is the same ownership level as in 1874 [100]

- Less than 2% of all U.S. farms are Black-owned

Residential Real Estate

- Since 1970, less than 2% of White homeowners have moved from predominantly White neighborhoods to predominantly Black neighborhoods

Business
Less than 2% of Black businesses have a presence in the following industries:

- Information Technology
- Finance and Insurance
- Manufacturing
- Agriculture
- Oil, Gas, and Mining
- Utilities
- Wholesale Trade

The Cumulative Effect of the Black Tax on African-American Wealth

The enormous cost of past discrimination against Black Americans, the current level of discrimination driven by explicit and implicit bias, and the low representation of African-Americans in critical careers, and industries as seen by the 2% phenomena has dramatically reduced the ability of Black Americans to accumulate wealth. Black American households currently have $8.4 trillion less wealth than they otherwise should have, which includes:

- $1.5 trillion less of retirement assets
- $2 trillion less of business equity
- $4.8 trillion less of primary home equity

And within the larger African-American community there are:
- 1.4 million[101] fewer Black businesses
- 6 million fewer jobs
- $1 trillion[102] less in business revenue
- $520 billion less in consumer income

In addition, the children of the White baby boomer generation are going to inherit approximately $30 trillion over the next several years—an amount that is 20 times the net worth of all Black Americans. This is why White Americans are significantly more likely to receive an inheritance, and when they do, those inheritances are vastly larger and more likely to increase their wealth profile.

Diversity/Minority Does Not Mean Black

The question is now, not if there is a Black tax, because clearly there is, but what can we do about it? How do we fill the massive gap of 6 million jobs, 1.4 million business and trillions of dollars of net worth? Many folks believe that a large part of the answer lies with increasing the size, scope, and effectiveness of various diversity and inclusion programs within corporations and governments. This is certainly a vitally important pathway, because these programs can dramatically increase minority presence on payrolls and in supply chains. A supply chain is comprised of the businesses that you purchase goods and services from to achieve your personal or business objectives. However, this must be done with caution because these programs and initiatives are built around the concept of increasing "diversity" and including "minorities" in various parts of the companies where they are underrepresented. However, "diversity" and "minority" do not mean Black. Diversity and minority are generally euphemisms for non-White males, which means a myriad of various other groups fall into these categories. Therefore, a company, entity or institution can have a very successful diversity or minority initiative with a marginal impact on Black employment and Black enterprises.

Consider the following statistics:

- Women-owned businesses with employees generated revenue of $1.2 trillion; less than 2% of that revenue was from Black women-owned businesses (88% White)

- Hispanic-owned businesses with employees generated revenue of $380 billion; less than 2% of that revenue was from Black-owned businesses (84% White)

- Asian-owned business with employees generated revenue of $628 billion; there are, by definition, zero Black-owned businesses in this category

- Black, Hispanic, and Asian "minority-owned banks" have $194 billion of assets, 2.5% of those assets are in Black-owned banks

To create jobs and to develop and expand business in the Black community, you must remember that minority and diversity do not mean Black, and your focus must be on efforts to increase Black participation in these programs. How can we do this?

Education is critically important but not sufficient.

Many people believe that dramatically increasing the post-secondary education level among African-Americans, (i.e., increasing the percentage of African-American bachelor degree holders) is the solution. While this is vitally important and has the potential to increase lifetime earnings by millions of dollars, post-secondary education attainment alone will not be sufficient. The main reason is that current and past anti-Black discrimination has led Blacks to have perpetually higher unemployment rates than Whites at every education level. According to Algernon Austin of the Economic Policy Institute, 85% of Blacks would need to have bachelor's degrees for Black Americans to have the same employment rate as White Americans. The power of the Black tax means that Black Americans would need an 85% rate of post-secondary college degree attainment to have the same employment rate as White Americans with a 36% rate of college degree attainment. While increasing Black bachelor degree holders from 24% to 85% would be a herculean effort, it would however, result in 2 million more Black Americans in the labor force. It would also cost African-Americans trillions of dollars to do so. Given that Black American college graduates occupy a disproportionately high percentage of low-earning occupations after college, they would be mired in hundreds of billions of dollars of debt combined with low-paying jobs, which would dramatically reduce their ability to accumulate wealth.

Move out of inner cities.

Some believe that as Blacks move out of inner cities into the suburbs that employment and other opportunities will increase significantly. While this may seem helpful, the reality is that as of 2010, 51% of Blacks in the 100 largest metro areas in the nation already live in the suburbs (which is four times the level in 1960) with no corresponding improvement in the employment rate for Black Americans over the past 60 years. This is because as Blacks moved into the suburbs closest to the inner cities, Whites moved further into the outer suburbs taking their economic and business resources with them. This left many Black suburbs with a limited economic base and even higher poverty levels than some inner cities.

Lobby for massive government action.

Others believe that massive government action, backed by the private sector is necessary to reverse the wealth and employment gap. While this is indeed true, the effects of massive government action, backed by the private sector, may be less impactful and long-lasting than expected, because the economic circulatory system within the Black community is almost nonexistent. This is because Black Americans (1) currently spend 98% of their income on non-Black-owned companies and service providers and (2) deposit 98% of the resources with non-Black-owned banks that serve the Black community. Therefore, massive government action, would almost certainly result in a massive stimulus for the non-Black enterprises that provide products and services to the Black community. Since these companies employ significantly fewer African-Americans than Black-owned companies and fund Black enterprises at far lower levels, such actions would likely lead to lower employment levels for Black Americans than would otherwise be the case if Black-owned businesses were the primary suppliers.

To maximize the employment levels and business development within the Black community, all of the strategies mentioned above (African-American inclusion and supplier programs, higher post-secondary education levels, safer communities with more economic opportunities and massive government and private sector actions) must be implemented together, not separately, and must rest on a foundation based on two new paradigms. The first new paradigm is centered on personal financial management at an individual and household level with a focus on Stewardship, Ownership, and Legacy (SOuL). This concept is covered thoroughly in Book 1 of my Financial Empowerment Series, CPR for the SOuL: How to Give Yourself a 20% Raise, Eliminate Your Debt and Leave an Inheritance for Your Children's Children. Stewardship is about getting the highest and best use out of the limited resources that you currently possess. It is about maximizing your household cash flow, because without cash flow, there's no savings, no assets, no investments, and no wealth to pass on. It's also about using your gifts and abilities to generate a significant return on your limited resources. Ownership is about the elimination of all claims on, or debts against, your assets, which in turn maximizes the amount of personal and or household cash flow available to you. Legacy is about (1) positioning yourself to leave an inheritance for your children's children, (2) having enough resources to retire with dignity, and (3) proactively setting aside money so you can help those in need. Due to the lack of financial management knowledge in African-American households and the impact of a debt-driven, consumer-driven society, a significant portion of African-American household income is consumed by debt payments and wasteful spending. A focus on stewardship, ownership, and legacy, which is about sacrificing short-term gratification for long-term transformation, will divert more resources to intergenerational wealth accumulation and wealth transfer.

Get Your P.H.D.

The second paradigm is centered on the concept of purchasing, hiring, and depositing within the Black community on a consumer, corporate, and public-sector level. PHD is an acronym for **Purchase, Hire,** and **Deposit**. Anyone who is interested in economic development within the broader African-American community should have, as a core part of their strategy, a focus on purchasing products and services from Black enterprises, hiring Black Americans into well-paying jobs, and depositing funds in Black financial institutions. A focus on PHD addresses the pervasive and devastating problem of African-Americans continually spending and depositing 98% of their resources outside of Black-owned financial and business enterprises, on businesses and enterprises which in turn do not purchase, hire and deposit into the Black community on any level. This cataclysmic combination has created a substantially depressive effect on employment, business creation and development, wealth creation, and financial and political independence in Black America.

To reduce the impact of the Black tax and create an environment that will facilitate the closing of the 6 million jobs gap and 1.4 million businesses gap in the Black community and $8 trillion of missing net worth, requires a foundation based on economic development and employment driven by the concept of "getting" your PHD. Getting your PHD is about facilitating trade and commerce with Black employees, businesses, and financial institutions to create a solid foundation for wealth accumulation. If Black enterprises are not represented in a company or institution's supply chain, Black employees are not represented on their payroll, or Black financial institutions are not represented where they deposit their money, not only are these businesses or enterprises not facilitating economic development (i.e., jobs and business development) in the African-American community, they are depressing it. To the extent that consumers, especially African-American consumers, and those who work toward or otherwise support the idea of job and business creation within the Black community, purchase, hire and deposit with Black enterprises, they will be able to have 100 times more impact on Black economic development than they otherwise would.

THE POWER OF PURCHASING

Consider the following statistics, which
represent trillions of dollars of spending:

- African-Americans spend 2% of their $1.2
  trillion spending power on Black businesses
- Corporations spend hundreds of billions
  on their supply chain and less than 2% of
  that purchasing power is spent with Black
  businesses
- The federal government spends close to $600
  billion annually buying goods and services
  from its suppliers and has a target of 5% of
  that earmarked for disadvantaged businesses.
  However, substantially less than 5% goes to
  Black businesses

Purchasing is about Consumers, Businesses, and Governments (CBGs) purchasing products and services from Black
enterprises. Whether you are a consumer, a business, or a government, if you are interested in creating jobs and businesses within the Black community, the purchasing of goods and
services from Black enterprises must be a priority within your
supply chain strategy. Remember: Your supply chain is comprised of the businesses that you purchase goods and services
from to achieve your personal or business objectives. Since
it is unwise to expect others to prioritize something that you
do not, you should make purchasing goods and services from
Black enterprises a priority. You should also encourage, and
whenever possible, require those with whom you do business
to also prioritize purchasing products and services from Black
enterprises. This is vitally important because the demand for

goods and services drives the need for employment (job creation) at existing businesses and the creation of new businesses to meet any excess demand. Since African-Americans and other CBGs spend less than 2% of their resources on African-American goods and services, a slight increase in demand could have a massive impact on job creation and business development.

The potential to stimulate job creation is far greater than most people understand. While it is widely known that Black consumers have a purchasing power of $1.2 trillion, what is not widely understood is that the economic impact of African-American purchasing power supports 24 million jobs in the U.S. economy. Unfortunately, almost all of the economic impact of that purchasing power (in terms of job creation and business development) occurs outside of the Black community, because African-American consumers spend less than 2% of their $1.2 trillion income on Black enterprises. To put this in perspective, U.S. consumers purchase 70% of all goods and services produced in America, while Black consumers spend under 2% of their income on services produced by Black businesses.

> **U.S. consumers purchase 70% of all goods and services produced in America, while Black consumers spend under 2% of their income on services produced by Black businesses.**

This is a huge missed opportunity because purchasing products and services from Black enterprises drives incremental employment within those enterprises and within their supplier base. This means that employees also make purchases from other companies that induce even more employment. For every additional job within a Black enterprise (direct employment), another job is created within their supply chain (indirect employment) and another is created from the economic activity of those employees (induced employment). Because Black enterprises have the highest concentration of Black employees, in most cases up to 75%[103] of those jobs will be from the Black community.

U.S. corporations spend hundreds of billions of dollars on their supply chains but only 2% of that spending is with Black companies. The federal government also purchases nearly $600 billion a year and has a target for 5% of that spending to go to disadvantaged businesses. Since many of the largest Black enterprises are suppliers of products and services in corporate and government supply chains, a greater representation of Black-owned businesses within corporate and government supply chains would stimulate massive demand for more employment within existing Black enterprises. It would also attract capital to form new businesses to meet any incremental, unmet demand. Since Black enterprises currently employ almost 1 million people, and Black representation in corporate and government supply chains is so low, even a small increase in demand could generate the need for 1 million to 2 million additional jobs.

THE POWER OF HIRING

Consider the following statistics:

- 93% of Black-owned businesses rely on 50% or more minorities to fill available jobs, while 60% of White small businesses have zero minority employees [104]

- African-Americans account for 2.7% of senior-level staff in the financial industry despite borrowing $150 billion per year to finance home and auto purchases

- Blacks are less than 2% (1%) of film executives and directors who are members of the Academy of Motion Picture Arts and Sciences membership, despite generating 13% of annual gross receipts or $1.3 billion a year

- Blacks make up about 2% of recent hires at tech firms despite being massive consumers of technology and social media

Overall, in terms of purchasing, African-Americans spend $1.2 trillion and support 24 million jobs in the U.S. economy. While many of these jobs are high-skilled and well-paying, few are held by African-Americans. There are assorted reasons for this; some are nefarious, like explicit bias, some are unintentional like implicit bias, others are due to the lack of social and professional networks. However, regardless of the cause, the impact is an extremely low representation of African-Americans within the payroll of many companies that depend on Black consumers. This low representation also depresses the earning power of large numbers of Black workers and reduces their ability to accumulate wealth.

Think of it this way: When you buy a good or service, you are engaging in trade, and the purpose of trade is to leave both parties in a better position than before the trade. If your community, region, or state is in need of investment, then your participation in trade should facilitate meeting that need. If you are the seller, you can use your profits to address the need. If you are a buyer, you can and should encourage the seller to invest in your economic development to secure your business.

If trading with you is profitable, then the seller will invest accordingly to secure your business. This is not the case with African-American consumers, because (1) African-Americans had never been allowed to impose any significant requirements on those who do business in our communities and (2) it has now become normal to

"People are more likely to change their behavior when they have an incentive to do so. If their jobs or profit margin is affected by their level of hiring African-Americans, they will have plenty of incentive to hire more."

trade without demanding or expecting more for our money, which is now over $1.2 trillion. To spend over $1 trillion per year and not expect or require meaningful investments in African-American economic development encourages exploitation, not investment. One of the most potent ways to spur economic development is through employment, which allows consumers to support their families, invest in their communities and consume more.

However, there are millions of African-Americans missing from the payrolls of various companies and institutions because there is little incentive to hire more African-Americans. As we have seen in Parts One and Two, bias against Black Americans is significant, long-lasting, and has mostly evolved from a conscious to subconscious state, so waiting for people to change on their own would not be a wise strategy. People are more likely to change their behavior when they have an incentive to do so. If their jobs or profit margin is affected by their level of hiring African-Americans, they will have plenty of incentive to hire more. It is also important to understand the power of marginal economics. Since the average company is not very profitable, (the average profit margins of most companies are between 3% to 4%) small changes in revenue can have a large effect on profitability. Therefore, changes in African-American spending patterns can have a significant impact on company profit margins. Our spending does matter and should be prioritized with companies that invest in us. When we spend money with a company, we should think about it as a form of investment, and in exchange for our investment, we should receive a quality product or service and they should also invest in us. One of the best ways to invest in a community is to employ people within that community.

THE POWER OF DEPOSITS

- 0.04% of all U.S. deposits or the equivalent of $4 out of every $10,000 deposited, is in Black-owned banks. If deposits in Black banks were proportional to the U.S. Black population, it would be closer to $1,400 out of every $10,000 ... instead of just $4 out of every $10,000

- To make matters worse, African-Americans deposit just 2% of their total deposits with Black-owned banks. Which leaves Black banks with an extremely limited ability to fund the growth and expansion of Black businesses. Meanwhile, Black businesses receive higher interest rates and higher denial rates than White businesses with the same credit

- Black, Hispanic, and Asian "minority-owned banks" have $194 billion of assets, 2.5% of those deposits are in Black-owned banks

- Black-owned small businesses received less than 2% (1.7%) of all loan money distributed through the SBA

To better understand the power of deposits, let's first look at banking. The banking system is the lifeblood of every economy. No country or state can be strong (financially secure) if it does not have a strong banking system. Banks collect and hold deposits from their customers and extend credit to businesses and individuals with those deposits. This process of holding deposits and providing loans creates additional money within the economy and is called the money multiplier effect. Think of it is this way: If you deposit $10 in a bank, the Federal

Reserve requires the bank to hold a certain portion in reserve. This means that there is a certain amount of the $10 deposit that the bank won't be able to lend and must keep on hand. The amount the bank has to keep on hand (or hold in reserve) is typically about 10%. This means, the bank can lend $9 of the $10 that was deposited. The person who receives the $9 loan will likely deposit that money into a bank, and that bank will be required to hold $0.90 in reserve and can lend $8.10 and so on and so forth.

In a well-functioning financial market, this process will continue until the initial $10 of deposits has led to the creation of $100 in incremental deposits. This can create a 10-times (or 10x) money-multiplier effect on every deposit. This is vitally important because African-Americans have over $130 billion deposited in various banks but only 2% is in Black-owned banks. While Black Americans could be creating a massive money-multiplier effect within the banking system, almost all of it is outside of the Black community. This starves Black businesses and consumers of much-needed capital, exposing them to the cost of implicit and explicit bias (the Black tax) in the financial system. And ultimately subsidizes the level of discrimination that Black businesses and consumers continually face.

The banking system generally works in the following way. Consumers, businesses, and governments (CBGs) make Deposits in banks, banks provide Credit (loans) for CBGs, CBGs spend money to fund their needs, this Spending stimulates Production, which in turn leads to Employment and employment creates more Deposits. In the U.S. economy, CBGs have $11 trillion of deposits within the banking system. Banks have made $15 trillion in loans to CBGs, CBGs spend $18.5 trillion, which supports 152 million civilian jobs. U.S. banks employ 2.1 million employees and are the circulatory system for the U.S. economy. This is why banks are bailed out during financial crises and consumers are left to fend for themselves.

There can be no transformative and sustainable economic development within the African-American community if Black Americans do not place deposits in their own banks and require others who wish to do business with them to do the same. If Black Americans moved their $130 billion of deposits to Black-owned banks, those banks would immediately have to hire 31,000 employees across many different departments (from IT, to sales, to human resources, to financial, to compliance, to tellers from top to bottom) and spend billions more to upgrade their facilities, IT infrastructure, and their supply chains. This would generate another 70,000 jobs within these supply chains. The net effect would be the creation of 100,000 new jobs, many of which can be sourced with Black talent. These Black banks would also be able to lend $120 billion to Black consumers, and businesses that need capital for homes, business expansion, and real-estate development. This would increase the capital available to Black businesses and consumers by 30 times and given that startup capital for Black enterprises has been funded almost exclusively by undercapitalized Blacks for almost 400 years, the impact would be a game changer. This would allow Black enterprises for the first time to have access to sufficient capital to truly compete and thrive through their full business life cycle (start up, ramp up, expand and mature).

To be clear, discrimination in credit markets on the basis of race and ethnicity is well-documented by researchers and is starving Black businesses of much-needed capital. So much so that only 6% of Black businesses say that their primary sources of credit come from banks. Less than 1% of Black businesses in a Pepperdine study were able to get a Small Business Administration-backed loan. A 2016 report from the Association for Enterprise Opportunity (AEO) found that (1) "80% of Black businesses desired financing for planned growth or expansion," (2) "73% of Black business owners indicate that the current business financing environment is restricting their ability to hire new employees," and (3) the funding gap in businesses loans for Black businesses could be almost $9 billion. Given that Black businesses currently employ almost 1 million people, if they received enough business loans to close this $9 billion gap, it could easily lead to the hiring of another 500,000 employees. This $9 billion funding gap could be closed in short order if African-Americans deposited a mere 10% of their deposits in Black banks.

If African-Americans had a well-functioning banking system where Black consumers, businesses, employees, institutions, and supply chains, along with CBGs that want to facilitate economic development within the Black community, deposited their money in Black banks, those deposits could create over $1 trillion of incremental lending and deposits (via the money multiplier effect).

This would also have the additional benefit of causing non-Black banks and financial institutions to compete for Black deposits and Black customers, which would cause them to put systems in place to reduce anti-Black bias and discrimination. These financial institutions would not tolerate discrimination against Black consumers and businesses regardless of the source, cause or intent (i.e., implicit or explicit bias) if the discrimination negatively affected their profit margins. ✪

By developing a full understanding of those factors that define one's relationship with one's adversary, and by actively controlling and shaping the situation so that the weaknesses of one's adversary are exposed to one's acquired strength, one is able to ride the forces of circumstance to victory.

— The Art of War, Sun Tzu

THE WAY FORWARD

The High Cost Of The Black Tax

n Part One: The Current Black Tax, we explored the current cost of implicit and explicit bias against Black Americans and found that the bias is pervasive, systematic, and the cost is significant. This tax exists in the housing market, where we saw that if you're Black (1) you're more likely be told about fewer homes and shown fewer homes when you are looking for a home. (2) You're also more likely to be treated as if your credit worthiness is substantially lower than it is if you have an African-American-sounding name. (3) You are 60% more likely to be turned down for a loan than Whites with similar characteristics. (4) You are three times more likely to receive a higher-priced loan than your White counterpart with the same credit risk. (5) Your home could end up being worth 18% less than it otherwise should be, if you live in an area where the Black population is more than 10% of the total population. And for a home purchased by an African-American for $450,000, the increased interest rate, fees and the long-term equity appreciation gap could cost an additional $345,000 over 30 years. *For Black Americans, the equity appreciation gap alone could be reducing their real estate holdings by $317 billion.*

We saw that a Black tax exists in the auto market where African-American buyers are more likely to: (1) Pay a higher purchase price, (2) Receive higher financing costs, (3) Get higher insurance premiums even if they have a perfect driving record but live in a Black community. This could cost up to $70,000 over the course of a buyer's life. Given that Black Americans purchase or lease about 5 million cars per year, the cumulative cost could be up to $10 billion per year in incremental automotive costs.

We saw that a Black tax exists in the online commerce market where an African-American-sounding name, a picture of a Black seller, or even the mere presence of Black fingers holding an item, can lower the value of what they are selling by 20% to 35%. In the job market, we saw that a resume with an African-American-sounding name can get 50% fewer callbacks for interviews than the same resume with a White-sounding name and requires up to eight more years of work experience to compensate for the Black-sounding name. In large law firms, partners will often find 100% more mistakes in legal memos if they believe that the author of the memo is a Black lawyer versus when they think the same memo is written by a White lawyer. They will also see less likelihood for future success as a lawyer when the same memo is thought to be written by a Black attorney—*the consequence of which can cost a promising Black lawyer $11 million in lifetime earnings.*

In Part Two: Historical Black Tax, we explored the economic value extracted from and denied to Black Americans during slavery and throughout the 150 years since slavery. We saw that the economic value extracted from enslaved people was $50 trillion and that the economic value of those people in 1860 was the equivalent of $22 trillion in today's dollars. *Blacks were emancipated from slavery with virtually no wealth, land, or means to sustain themselves, while White families were given 246 million acres worth up to $1.5 trillion.* Black Americans were then quickly forced into a Jim Crow segregation period, which stripped them of another $15 trillion over the next 65 years. During this time, they were subjected to an ill-funded, inferior educational system, *which reduced their earning power by 50% for several generations.* Blacks received less than 2% of the trillion-dollar stimuli associated with the New Deal, the G.I. Bill, and the VA/FHA housing programs.

Black Americans were denied mortgages, and denied the ability to live in safe, prosperous neighborhoods occupied by Whites, which cost future generation almost $5 trillion in equity. We saw the systematic discrimination, supported by law and custom, that denied Blacks access to almost all high-paying, high-skill jobs and careers and high-quality education *for almost 100 years.* This saddled African-Americans with high unemployment, high poverty, high crime, and a high incarnation rate. They were then ill-prepared for the shift from an economy driven by manufacturing jobs to one driven by high-skill service jobs. *We saw that the end result of this massive economic disenfranchise-*

ment, this Black tax, is having $8 trillion less wealth than we otherwise should, there being 6 million fewer jobs employed by Black businesses and 1.4 million fewer Black businesses with employees than we should have.

The Power of PHD and SOuL

In Part Three: What Can We Do About the Black Tax? We learned powerful strategies to reduce and eventually eliminate the effects of the Black tax. The most vital is that we should get our PHD, which is to (1) Purchase, Hire, and Deposit Black and (2) practice Stewardship, Ownership, and Legacy (SOuL). At this point, there is misalignment between what we say we want and where our actions and resources are invested. African-Americans want economic empowerment and financial independence but our actions and resources are collectively invested in things that (1) will not bring that about and (2) often work against us. Societies are built on communities and communities are built on families and families are built on the means to generate income to support their basic needs and allocate any excess to wealth accumulation. If we want to create jobs to sustain and elevate families then PHD is necessary. If we want to create intergenerational wealth at an individual level then stewardship, ownership, and legacy (SOuL) is necessary. If we want to have a strong political base to limit future disenfranchisement, then both are needed.

As we've seen, the concept of PHD is simple and powerful: We should *Purchase, Hire,* and *Deposit* in Black businesses, banks, and communities. It is vitally important that African-Americans lead by example, because it is foolish to expect others to invest more in us than we are willing to invest in ourselves. We should also require CBGs that we do business with to get their PHD as well. At the end of the day, our actions matter. If our actions are consistent with PHD, they will facilitate significant incremental economic development in the form of job creation, business development, and wealth accumulation. Nelson Mandela, the first president of South Africa after the fall of Apartheid once said that "our attitudes to [others] are based on their attitudes to our struggles," therefore it makes strategic sense to invest in, partner with, and otherwise support institutions and policies that drive PHD. PHD is powerful because it links capital and employment and the demand for goods and services. It is also self-reinforcing, because PHD (1) increases deposits which provides the capital to fund business formation and expansion (i.e., product development, human capital acquisition and development, management systems, sales and marketing;) (2) stimulates additional hiring within both Black and non-Black enterprises and their supply chains, which also increases deposits; and (3) stimulates purchases at the consumer, corporate, and government levels via supply chain spending and personal consumption.

Businesses generally fail because of a lack of capital and lack of demand for their goods and services. This is also the case for Black businesses. Black enterprises have historically had extremely limited access to all forms of capital, and limited ability to trade freely by law, custom and extreme discrimination. However, the *African-American consumer market (along with other consumers who believe in African economic development) collectively have enough capital in the form of deposits and internal demand in the form of consumption, to provide a secure economic base for millions of Black businesses to grow and expand into larger and more diverse regional, national, and international markets.* This will, in turn, drive significant demand for hiring at all functional levels within those companies and within the African-American community.

Focusing on Stewardship, Ownership, and Legacy (SOuL) and getting your PHD not only reduces the effects of the Black tax, but also (1) focuses the mind on, and orients actions toward, things that stimulate capital, employment, and business development; (2) provides increased Opportunity, for Trade, Industry and Innovation, Capital, Skill and Security; (3) provides an important step toward repairing the damage from the Black tax. If you want to eliminate the gap of the 6 million jobs, 1.4 million businesses and $8 trillion of net worth missing from Black communities then you should start by getting your PHD, doing business with people, businesses and organizations that have their PHD, and supporting policies that drive PHD.

This is not a call to "support" Black enterprises, because "support" implies an uneven exchange with one side receiving and one giving. This is the charity mindset that many people have when they think about engaging with Black businesses, organizations and causes. *Black enterprises don't need your support; they need your business and you need the jobs that they will generate and the independence and wealth that those jobs will create. In exchange for your business, they will provide you with high-quality goods and services.* This will lead to a positive feedback loop that creates the need for more jobs, requires additional skills, demands more capital, induces more innovation, develops the economies of scale, which lowers prices, provides incomes for families, drives additional consumption, allows for wealth accumulation, and ultimately leaves a legacy for the next generation.

Black enterprises need the same things that predominantly White enterprises have received for 400 years which is a local, regional, and national commitment to their growth and continual success (including but not limited to low cost of capital, access to important markets, government investment, and government-friendly policies) in the global marketplace.

There is more than enough demand within the African-American community for Black businesses to flourish and serve as a base for them to expand into various regional, national, and global markets.

"There is more than enough demand within the African-American community for Black businesses to flourish and serve as a base for them to expand into various regional, national, and global markets."

I've heard many Black people express significant concerns about doing business with Black enterprises. If you have ever had a bad experience with a Black business, remember that (1) we also have biases against our own businesses and as such we tend to attribute localized negative experiences to "Black businesses" in general and (2) since there are 2.6 million Black businesses in America our personal experience is in no way representative of the quality of Black enterprises as a whole. I would encourage everyone to apply an equal amount of focus on the massive "cost" of *not* doing business with Black enterprises and remember that most world-class businesses took many decades to reach that status. But, they did it with significant preferential government support, access to capital along with unrestricted trade and development in their regional and national markets, all of which were intentionally denied to Black enterprises for hundreds of years.

In reality no business or industry in America has experienced the magnitude of exclusion and economic isolation (in terms of length of time and scale), *on every level vital to growth and success* as Black businesses. Despite that monumental level of discriminatory treatment, Black companies (1) employ about 1 million people across the nation, (2) are more diverse than all other businesses in America, (3) have invested enormous resources in the Black community when no one else would, and (4) have not had the predatory and discriminatory relationship that has cost the Black community over $70 trillion of denied and or extracted resources, resulting in 1.4 million fewer businesses, 6 million fewer jobs, and $8 trillion of net worth. Remember that as consumers, even though we spend 98% of our income on non-Black businesses, the mere knowledge of you being Black is enough to trigger (consciously or unconsciously) anti-Black bias, which can dramatically:

❒ Reduce your prospects of getting a callback for a job (regardless of the quality of your work experience)

❒ Increase the scrutiny of your work product and possibly reduce your long-term career trajectory

❒ Increase the likelihood that you will be denied credit for your business (even if your credit profile qualifies you to get the loan)

❒ Increase the likelihood that you will pay higher purchase prices and interest rates for cars (even if your credit profile qualifies you for a lower rate)

❐ Increase the likelihood that you will have to pay higher interest rates for home and business loans (even if your credit profile qualifies you for a lower rate)

❐ Reduce value of homes in areas where there are too many people who look like you (regardless of their income, wealth, or quality of the neighborhood)

❐ Lower the value of products that you sell online

...all of which serves as a massive Black tax that continues to cost African-Americans hundreds of billions of dollars each year and devastates our ability to leave a legacy. At the end of the day, the same amount of energy and effort that went into facilitating the current and historical Black tax must be invested in eliminating it and repairing the damage it caused. Given the enormity, longevity and pervasiveness of this Black tax, we must do as the Rev. Dr. Martin Luther King Jr. said in 1968, in his now famous "I've been to the mountain top" speech[105]: "Always anchor our external direct action with the power of economic withdrawal.", "begin the process of building a greater economic base," "deposit in Black banks," "buy from Black insurance companies," "redistribute the pain," and "strengthen Black institutions." This is vitally important because in the words of A.G. Gaston, one of the wealthiest, most successful and prolific African-American entrepreneurs of the 20th century, "we cannot fight and beg from those we fight with at the same time."

Therefore, arm yourself with the information and strategies in this book. Use them to create intergenerational change, build a foundation for economic development, provide jobs and income for families and communities. *To maximize your effectiveness, you must always remember to (1) focus on*

Stewardship, Ownership, and Legacy in your household (2) get your PHD, (3) encourage others to do the same (4) engage and patronize organizations and businesses that have their PHD, and (5) support policies that drive Purchasing, Hiring, and Deposits within the Black community. The time is now, and with your newly acquired PHD and your focus on Stewardship, Ownership, and Legacy, you will be ready to be the architect of a new day and to create a new legacy for your children's children. ✪

All things and events that have a distinguishing shape or disposition can be named, and all things that can be named can be prevailed over
— The Art of War, Sun Tzu

ABOUT THE AUTHOR

Shawn D. Rochester is an expert in identifying, optimizing, and allocating cash flow to help individuals, families, and organizations achieve their long-term financial goals. Shawn is a former corporate development and strategy executive who developed world-class cash flow management skills identifying and executing $500 million worth of transactions around the world and helping global business leaders generate over $10 billion of incremental revenue and cash flow.

Shawn spent the last 20 years developing The Good Steward Financial Empowerment Series. Its powerful financial principles, based on stewardship, ownership, and legacy, have helped individuals and families dramatically increase their ability to maximize their cash flow, eliminate their debt and leave a legacy not only for their children, but also for their children's children. Shawn and his wife, Delores founded Good Steward LLC (GSL) to provide financial education and advisory services based on the three core principles of stewardship, ownership, and legacy. Since founding GSL, Shawn has helped clients eliminate millions of dollars of debt, add tens of millions of assets to their retirement plans and position themselves to leave a greater legacy for their children's children, than many clients thought possible.

Shawn holds a bachelor's degree in Chemical Engineering from The University of Rochester, and a master's degree in Business Administration from The University of Chicago Booth School of Business with a focus in Accounting, Finance, and Entrepreneurship. He lives in Southbury, Connecticut, with his wife and two children.

The Black Tax: The Cost of Being Black in America is available at www.BlackTaxed.com

Visit www.BlackTaxed.com to purchase additional copies and share your personal Black Tax story.

Email the author at **shawn.rochester@goodstewardllc.com**

Follow me on Facebook: **GoodStewardLiving**
Follow me on Twitter: **rochester_shawn**
Follow me Instagram: **shawn.rochester**
www.GoodStewardLiving.com

RESOURCES & REFERENCES

[1] Hansona, Andrew and Zackary Hawley, Hal Martin, Bo Liu. "Discrimination in Mortgage Lending: Evidence from a Correspondence Experiment," *Journal of Urban Economics,* March 2016.

[2] Hansona, Andrew and Zackary Hawley, Hal Martin, Bo Liu. "Discrimination in Mortgage Lending: Evidence from a Correspondence Experiment," *Journal of Urban Economics,* March 2016, p. 62.

[3] Munnell, Alicia H. and Lynn Elaine Browne, James McEneaney, and Geoffrey M.B. Tootell, "Mortgage Lending in Boston: Interpreting the HMDA Data No.92-7," Federal Reserve Bank of Boston, October 1992, p. 2.

[4] http://www.epi.org/publication/bp335-boa-countrywide-discriminatory-lending/

[5] http://www.nytimes.com/2012/07/13/business/wells-fargo-to-settle-mortgage-discrimination-charges.html

[6] https://www.forbes.com/sites/forbesleadershipforum/2012/12/10/how-home-ownership-keeps-blacks-poorer-than-whites/#70324a1b4cce

[7] Squires, Gregory D. and Charis E. Kubrin, "Privileged Places: Race, Uneven Development and the Geography of Opportunity in Urban America," January 1, 2005, p. 51.

[8] Krysan, Maria, University of Illinois at Chicago and Mick P. Couper, University of Michigan, Reynolds Farley, University of Michigan, Tyrone Forman Emory University, "Does Race Matter in Neighborhood Preferences? Results from a Video Experiment."

[9] Emerson, Michael O. and Karen J. Chai and George Yancey, "Does Race Matter in Residential Segregation? Exploring the Preferences of White Americans," *American Sociological Review,* Vol. 66, No. 6, December 2001, pp. 922-935.

[10] http://www.socialworktoday.com/news/dn_060412.shtml

[11] Bruenig, Matt, "The Top 10% Of White Americans Own Almost Everything," September 5, 2014, http://www.demos.org/

blog/9/5/14/top-10-white-families-own-almost-everything.

[12] Ayres, Ian and Peter Siegelman, "Race and Gender Discrimination in Bargaining for a New Car," *The American Economic Review*, Vol. 85, No. 3, June 1995, pp. 304-321.

[13] "Racial Disparities in Auto Loan Markups State-by-State Data," National Consumer Law Center, June 2015.

[14] https://hbr.org/2016/12/fixing-discrimination-in-online-marketplaces

[15] "Race Effects on eBay," *The RAND Journal of Economics*, Vol. 46, No. 4, Winter 2015, pp. 891–917.

[16] Bertrand, Marianne and Sendhil Mullainathan, "Are Emily and Brendan More Employable Than Lakisha and Jamal? A Field Experiment in Labor Market Discrimination," *The American Economic Review*, Vol. 94, No. 4, September 2004, pp. 991-1013.

[17] Austin, Algernon, "A Jobs-Centered Approach to African American Community Development," Economic Policy Institute, Briefing Paper #328, December, 14, 2011, p. 5.

[18] Decker, Scott H. and Cassia Spohn, Ph.D. Natalie R. Ortiz, M.S., "Criminal Stigma, Race, Gender, and Employment: An Expanded Assessment of the Consequences of Imprisonment for Employment," U.S. Department of Justice, Document No. 244756, Received January 2014.

[19] Dan P Ly, doctoral student, Seth A Seabury, associate professor, Anupam B Jena, Ruth L Newhouse associate professor, "Differences in incomes of physicians in the United States by race and sex: observational study" British Medical Journal BMJ 2016;353:i2923

[20] https://www.ache.org/pubs/research/Report_Tables_Exec-Sum.pdf

[21] Blanchflower, David G. and Phillip B. Levine, David J. Zimmerman, "Discrimination in the Small Business Credit Market," NBER Working Paper No. 6840, December 1998.

[22] Robb, Alicia, Marin Consulting, LLC., "Access to Capital Among Young Firms, Minority-Owned Firms, Women-Owned Firms, and High-Tech Firms," Office of Advocacy, the United

States Small Business Administration, April 2013.

[23] "U.S. Dept. of Commerce Fact Sheet, African American Owned Firms," Minority Business Development Agency.

[24] https://thinkprogress.org/black-small-business-owners-get-left-out-of-loans-3c7fc0d05b2d

[25] Everett, Craig, Ph.D., Pepperdine Private Capital Access Index, Second Quarter 2016, Pepperdine/Graziadio School of Business Management.

[26] Oliver, Melvin L. Oliver and Thomas M. Shapiro, *Black Wealth/ White Wealth: A New Perspective on Racial Equality*, Routledge; 2nd edition, 2006, pp. 36–50.

[27] The percent figure was calculated by Fogel from Soltow: Robert W. Fogel, "A Comparison between the Value of Slave Capital in the Share of Total British Wealth (c.1811) and in the Share of Total Southern Wealth (c.1860)," chapter 56 of Robert William Fogel, Ralph A. Galantine, and Richard L. Manning, Without Consent or Contract: Evidence and Methods (New York: Norton, 1992); source: https://www.measuringworth.com/slavery.php

[28] Einhorn, Robin L., American Taxation, American Slavery, University of Chicago Press: 2006; Piketty, Thomas, Capital in the Twenty-First Century, Belknap Press: 2014.

[29] Smith, Andre L., Tax Law and Racial Economic Justice: Black Tax (Kindle version), Lexington Books: 2015, p. 92 of 213.

[30] Feagin, Joe R., "Documenting the Costs of Slavery, Segregation, and Contemporary Racism: Why Reparations Are in Order for African Americans," Harvard BlackLetter Law Journal, Vol. 20, Spring 2004, p. 55.

[31] https://newrepublic.com/article/117856/academic-evidence-reparations-costs-are-limited

[32] http://www.pbs.org/wnet/african-americans-many-rivers-to-cross/history/the-truth-behind-40-acres-and-a-mule/

[33] Feagin, Joe R., "Documenting the Costs of Slavery, Segregation, and Contemporary Racism: Why Reparations Are in Order for African Americans," Harvard BlackLetter Law Journal, Vol. 20, Spring 2004, p. 74.

[34] Walker, Juliette K., Encyclopedia of African American Business History, Greenwood: 1999, p. 251.

[35] Williams, Trina, "The Homestead Act: A Major Asset-Building Policy in American History," Working Paper No. 00-9, Center for Social Development (Washington University), September 2000, pp. 5–6.

[36] https://www.usda.gov/nass/PUBS/TODAYRPT/land0815.pdf

[37] Downs, James T., Sick from Freedom: African-American Illness and Suffering during the Civil War and Reconstruction, Oxford University Press: 2012.

[38] Taylor, Carol M., W.E.B Dubois's Challenge to Scientific Racism, Journal of Black Studies, Vol. 11, No. 4, June 1981, p. 451

[39] Statistical Abstract of the United States: 1999, 20th Century Statistics, U.S. Census Bureau, p. 874.

[40] https://www.theatlantic.com/business/archive/2014/12/empire-of-cotton/383660/

[41] Carter, Susan B., "Labor for Historical Statistics of the United States, Millennial Edition," University of California, Riverside, September 2003, p. 12,

[42] https://www.gilderlehrman.org/history-by-era/reconstruction/resources/sharecropper-contract-1867

[43] Blackmon, Douglas A., Slavery By Another Name: The Re-Enslavement of Black Americans From the Civil War to World War II, Doubleday: 2008, pp 67-68.

[44] Nier, Charles Lewis, III, "The Shadow of Credit: The Historical Origins of Racial Predatory Lending and its Impact Upon African American Wealth Accumulation, University of Pennsylvania Journal of Law and Social Change, Vol. 11, p. 161.

[45] Roback, Jennifer, "Exploitation in the Jim Crow South: The Market or the Law?," AEI Journal on Government and Society, 1984.

[46] Roback, Jennifer, "Exploitation in the Jim Crow South: The Market or the Law?," AEI Journal on Government and Society, 1984.

[47] Blackmon, Douglas A., Slavery By Another Name: The Re-Enslavement of Black Americans From the Civil War to World War II, Doubleday: 2008, p. 27.

[48] Blackmon, Douglas A., Slavery By Another Name: The Re-Enslavement of Black Americans From the Civil War to World War II, Doubleday: 2008, p. 27.

[49] Smith, Andre L., Tax Law and Racial Economic Justice: Black Tax (Kindle version), Lexington Books: 2015, p. 104.

[50] Jenkins, Carol and Elizabeth Gardner Hines, Black Titan; A.G. Gaston and the Making of a Black Millionaire, One World: 2005.

[51] Becker, Gary S., The Economics of Discrimination, Second Edition, p. 22.

[52] $31 million inflated at 3% per year from 1930 to 2017.

[53] U.S. Census Bureau (1933, Table 12, p. 24).

[54] https://www.thenation.com/article/violence-and-economic-mobility-jim-crow-south/

[55] Blecher, Cornell, A Black Man in the White House: Barack Obama and the Triggering of America's Racial Aversion Crisis, Kindle Edition

[56] https://www.cato.org/publications/commentary/why-did-fdrs-new-deal-harm-blacks

[57] http://www.digitalhistory.uh.edu/disp_textbook.cfm?smtID=2&psid=3447

[58] Perea, Juan F., "The Echoes of Slavery: Recognizing the Racist Origins of the Agricultural and Domestic Worker Exclusion," National Labor Relations Act

[59] Stoesz, David, "The Excluded: An Estimate of the Consequences of Denying Social Security to Agricultural and Domestic Workers" CSD Working Paper No. 16-17, 2016, p. 9.

[60] Swinton, David H., Racial Inequality and Reparations, in The Wealth of Races: The Present Value of Benefits From Past Injustices, edited by Richard F. America, Greenwood Press:1990, p. 156.

[61] https://mobile.nytimes.com/2005/08/28/books/review/

when-affirmative-action-was-white-uncivil-rights.html

[62] https://mobile.nytimes.com/2005/08/28/books/review/
when-affirmative-action-was-white-uncivil-rights.html

[63] https://mobile.nytimes.com/2005/08/28/books/review/
when-affirmative-action-was-white-uncivil-rights.html

[64] https://mobile.nytimes.com/2005/08/28/books/review/
when-affirmative-action-was-white-uncivil-rights.html

[65] Mason, Herman "Skip," Jr., The Talented Tenth, The Founders and Presidents of Alpha, p. 401; Jones, Eugene Kinckle, "The Negroes, North and South—A Contrast," Missionary View of the World, June 1922.

[66] Gibson, Campbell and Kay Jung, Historical Census Statistics on Population Totals By Race, 1790 to 1990, And By Hispanic Origin, 1970 to 1990, For Regions, Divisions, and States, Working Paper No. 6, 2002.

[67] The 14th Census: 1920; Summary For The United States, By Geographic Divisions And States.

[68] Anderson, James D., The Education of Black in the South, 1860–1935 (Kindle version), The University of North Carolina Press: 1988, p. 156 of 366.

[69] Anderson, James D., The Education of Black in the South, 1860–1935 (Kindle version), The University of North Carolina Press: 1988, p. 155 of 366.

[70] Margo, Robert A., Race and Schooling in the South, 1880-1950: An Economic History, University of Chicago Press, 1990, Chapter 2, p. 21.

[71] Bayer, Patrick and Kerwin Kofi Charles, "Divergent Paths: Structural Change, Economic Rank, and the Evolution of Black-White Earnings Differences, 1940-2014," NBER Working Paper No. 22797, p.32.

[72] Walker, Juliette K., Encyclopedia of African American Business History, Greenwood: 1999, p. 74.

[73] Carruthers, Celeste K. and Marianne H. Wanamaker, Separate and Unequal in the Labor Market: Human Capital and the Jim Crow Wage Gap, NBER Working Paper No. 21947, January 2016.

[74] Evans, Brian R. and Jacqueline Leonard, "Recruiting and Retaining Black Teachers to Work in Urban Schools," September 2013.

[75] Evans, Brian R. and Jacqueline Leonard, "Recruiting and Retaining Black Teachers to Work in Urban Schools," September 2013.

[76] Educational Research Service, "National Survey of Salaries and Wages [Paid Professional and Support Personnel] in Public Schools, 2005-06."

[77] Collier, Marta D., "Changing the Face of Teaching: Preparing Educators for Diverse Settings," Teacher Education Quarterly, Winter 2002.

[78] Lipsitz, George, A Life In The Struggle: Ivory Perry and the Culture of Opposition, Temple University Press: 1995, p. 27.

[79] Nier, Charles Lewis, III, "The Shadow of Credit: The Historical Origins of Racial Predatory Lending and its Impact Upon African American Wealth Accumulation, University of Pennsylvania Journal of Law and Social Change, Vol. 11, p. 183.

[80] Nier, Charles Lewis, III, "The Shadow of Credit: The Historical Origins of Racial Predatory Lending and its Impact Upon African American Wealth Accumulation, University of Pennsylvania Journal of Law and Social Change, Vol. 11, p.183.

[81] Nier, Charles Lewis, III, "The Shadow of Credit: The Historical Origins of Racial Predatory Lending and its Impact Upon African American Wealth Accumulation, University of Pennsylvania Journal of Law and Social Change, Vol. 11, p. 185.

[82] Nier, Charles Lewis, III, "The Shadow of Credit: The Historical Origins of Racial Predatory Lending and its Impact Upon African American Wealth Accumulation, University of Pennsylvania Journal of Law and Social Change, Vol. 11, p. 181.

[83] http://time.com/3942084/jackie-robinson-racial-progress/

[84] Kopf, Dan, "The Great Migration: The African American Exodus from The South" Priceonomics, January 28, 2016.

[85] http://www.chicagotribune.com/business/ct-contract-sell-ing-resurgence-20160513-story.html m

[86] Becker, Gary S., The Economics of Discrimination, Second Edition, p. 28.

[87] http://www.pbs.org/newshour/making-sense/todays-racial-wealth-gap-is-wider-than-in-the-1960s/

[88] "The 'Greater' Wealth Transfer: Capitalizing on the Intergenerational Shift in Wealth," Accenture Wealth and Asset Management Services, June 2012.

[89] Bayer, Patrick and Kerwin Kofi Charles, "Divergent Paths: Structural Change, Economic Rank, and the Evolution of Black-White Earnings Differences, 1940-2014," NBER Working Paper No. 22797, p. 3.

[90] Darity, William, Jr., "Forty Acres and a Mule: Placing a Price Tag on Oppression," The Wealth of Races: The Present Value of Benefits From Past Injustices, edited by Richard F. America, New York: Greenwood Press, 1990.

[91] Bayer, Patrick and Kerwin Kofi Charles, "Divergent Paths: Structural Change, Economic Rank, and the Evolution of Black-White Earnings Differences, 1940-2014," NBER Working Paper No. 22797, Table 1.

[92] Whitehead, Tony L., "The Formation of the U.S. Racialized Urban Ghetto," The Cultural Systems Analysis Group (CuSAG) Special Problems Working Paper Series in Urban Anthropology, The University of Maryland, September 15, 2000, p. 8.

[93] Whitehead, Tony L., "The Formation of the U.S. Racialized Urban Ghetto," The Cultural Systems Analysis Group (CuSAG) Special Problems Working Paper Series in Urban Anthropology, The University of Maryland, September 15, 2000, p. 8.

[94] Bayer, Patrick and Kerwin Kofi Charles, "Divergent Paths: Structural Change, Economic Rank, and the Evolution of Black-White Earnings Differences, 1940-2014," NBER Working Paper No. 22797, Table 6.

[95] Bayer, Patrick and Kerwin Kofi Charles, "Divergent Paths: Structural Change, Economic Rank, and the Evolution of Black-White Earnings Differences, 1940-2014," NBER Working Paper No. 22797, Table 6.

[96] "Statistical Brief: Black Americans," U.S. Census Bureau, March 1993.

[97] Blecher, Cornell, A Black Man in the White House: Barack Obama and the Triggering of America's Racial Aversion Crisis, Kindle Edition, Location 1564 of 2602.

[98] http://www.vox.com/2014/6/27/5847194/only-7-per-cent-of-conservatives-say-racial-discrimination-holds-back

[99] Blecher, Cornell, A Black Man in the White House: Barack Obama and the Triggering of America's Racial Aversion Crisis, Kindle Edition, Location 1564 of 2602.

[100] Table 68, 1999 Agricultural Economics and Land Ownership Survey.

[101] "U.S. Dept. of Commerce Fact Sheet, African American Owned Firms," Minority Business Development Agency.

[102] "U.S. Dept. of Commerce Fact Sheet, African American Owned Firms," Minority Business Development Agency.

[103] Walker, Juliette E.K., Encyclopedia of African American Business History, p. 200.

[104] Walker, Juliette E.K., Encyclopedia of African American Business History, p. 200.

[105] http://www.americanrhetoric.com/speeches/mlkivebeento-themountaintop.htm